THE
METACOGNITION
HANDBOOK

A PRACTICAL GUIDE FOR TEACHERS AND SCHOOL LEADERS

JENNIFER WEBB

First Published 2021

by John Catt Educational Ltd,
15 Riduna Park, Station Road,
Melton, Woodbridge IP12 1QT

Tel: +44 (0) 1394 389850
Email: enquiries@johncatt.com
Website: www.johncatt.com

ISBN: 978 1 91362 253 4

Set and designed by John Catt Educational Limited

This book is for all the incredible women who speak into my life.

My aunties, my trailblazing nana, my perfectly imperfect mum.

To Louise, who reminds me that my work is just part of a bigger puzzle.

To PLN Group 2 – the ladies in my back pocket – thank you for being fierce.

To WomenEd, the Maternity CPD Project and the online teaching community, thank you for being positive disrupters.

Praise for 'The Metacognition Handbook'

The Metacognition Handbook transforms a complex concept and makes it manageable and meaningful for teachers. It is a book for teachers looking to make a difference in their classrooms and leaders seeking to support implementing metacognition with success. Webb distils a wealth of research evidence, useable tools and practical case studies in such an accessible style that it makes this book required reading.

Alex Quigley (@HuntingEnglish), teacher, blogger and author of *Closing the Reading Gap*

Jennifer has achieved her aim in writing a book rooted in academic research that focuses on the practical guidance for classroom teachers and leaders. Metacognition has certainly generated a lot of interest in recent years but often lacked the much-needed clarity that Jennifer brings in *The Metacognition Handbook*. There are CPD experiences and classroom scenarios that all teachers will relate to, followed by golden nuggets of advice, suggestions and solutions throughout. Plentiful examples are provided in a digestible format and with fascinating insight. This book has made me reflect and think differently about metacognition as well as provide strategies for me to implement in my own classroom and embed as a middle leader.

Kate Jones (@KateJones_teach) is the author of *Love To Teach* **and the** *Retrieval Practice* **collection, in addition to her teaching and leadership role at The British School Al Khubairat, Abu Dhabi**

The Metacognition Handbook is rich in research which Jennifer has unlocked expertly to provide clarity for busy teachers and leaders. It is accompanied by an array of practical classroom strategies that can be implemented with clear guidance on how it will support pupils. Highly recommended.

Michael Chiles (m_chiles), teacher, Director of Tech and Innovation at @KingsWoolston, author of *The CRAFT of Assessment* and *The Feedback Pendulum* and Chartered College of Teaching council member

Contents

Contents

Foreword
by Peps Mccrea and Louise Saukila

What an incredible time to be a teacher. Sure, there have been a few tricky challenges to navigate recently (what an understatement), but when we step back and look at the capacity of our profession to tackle our most pressing task – helping pupils to learn – then things have never looked better.

Teachers in the UK, and increasingly beyond, are having some of the most rigorous and passionate conversations the profession has ever seen. Evidence from research is more plentiful than ever before, open access movements are driving access in unprecedented ways, and the effort to translate empirical findings into practices in ways that can be deployed with fidelity in the classroom – a critical part of the improvement ecosystem – is bourgeoning.

Cognition, or 'thinking', is both a central focus of this work, and one of the most complex processes the universe has ever seen. However, when we start to dig into 'thinking about thinking' – metacognition – we're straying into some of the most ambitious territory the sector has ever grappled with.

With this in mind, it's little surprise that the science around metacognition is far from settled yet. Debate continues around what it is, the extent to which we can influence it, and whether it even exists as a meaningfully separate concept. As a profession, we welcome this debate, it is an essential cornerstone of scientific progress and one we should increasingly seek to appreciate. But we also can't wait around for it to be fully settled. There are pupils in classrooms ready to learn now and so I think it is only sensible to be exploring potential application, albeit with caution.

Which is why it's such a huge delight to 'cut the ribbon' for *The Metacognition Handbook*. In this book, as a prime example of the endeavours of our era, Jennifer interrogates the evidence from a teacher's perspective, provides a framework for thinking about metacognition, and offers a range of highly practical strategies that she and fellow colleagues have tried, tested and iterated in authentic school contexts. And so, if you are on a similar journey to further understand and wrestle with how the evidence might be harnessed in service of learning, particularly for one of the most complex topics in the game (maybe even the universe), then you should find this book to be a worthy companion.

Hats off to Jennifer for writing this and to the rest of you for reading it.

Yours in getting better,

Peps

Peps Mccrea, Dean at Ambition Institute and author of the *High Impact Teaching* series, pepsmccrea.com

∗∗

The brain and its ability and capacity to learn never ceases to amaze. I often consider this as I reflect on my journey of understanding the brain and its functions and disruptions whilst pursuing my career as a neurosurgeon. Having an understanding of the brain, how it learns, and how this can change over time drives the concept of metacognition. This is by no means a new idea, with writings relating to metacognition dating back to Aristotle, but this underused tool has the ability to transform classroom environments into much happier and optimised places for learning.

As a brain surgeon, I view learning from a unique perspective. When making career choices at the age of 17, I was drawn to the brain and the wonder of how it could withstand surgical tamper without impact on a person's function and mind. It was at this point that I decided on my career path. My highlights of medical school were all focused on learning about the brain. From the excitement of spending hours interrogating brain prosection specimens, learning neuroanatomy, conducting experiments to gain understanding of neurophysiological processes and neuropsychology, to my favourite specialist clinical attachments in neurology and neurosurgery, the brain truly fascinated me. My continued pursuit of a career in neurosurgery was clear and I have now been training in this field for a decade.

It was during my student years that I met Jennifer through our shared passion for music, but it was as first-time mothers (just days apart) that we were reunited, with our friendship since evolving. Our time on maternity leave together allowed us to discuss at length the highlights and challenges of our chosen careers. I quickly gained an appreciation for Jennifer's passion for education and improving the way English is taught, with a wonderful desire to bring a freshness and vibrancy to the classroom to engage all students. Conversations considered the challenges of accessibility, individualised learning needs and requirements, and improving and expanding on the diversity of texts studied to make them more relevant and reflective of modern society. In response I would share personal insights into some of the incredible feats that can be achieved with neurosurgery, with remarkable patient recoveries and the ability of the brain to learn and relearn following significant insult.

I view the brain from a privileged vantage point, with a subsequent front-row seat to what happens when the brain is disrupted and the impact on a patient. Disturbances of the brain have taught us more about how we learn and how storage of learning can change and evolve over time. Let us consider language. How we store and process the language of our mother tongue is completely different to that of a foreign language learned later in life. This is sometimes exemplified by the impact of head injury in which the ability to speak a foreign language may become temporarily or sometimes permanently lost whilst speech in the mother tongue remains intact. This does not hold true if the patient is truly bilingual, having learned both languages together at an early age.

We use our awareness of the incredible ability of the brain to not only learn but to move where that learning is stored when planning tumour surgery in functionally eloquent parts of the brain. In such cases, awake surgery with functional testing can allow partial tumour resection without functional impairment. Although part of the tumour is left behind, experience has taught us that repeat surgery just months later, with repeat functional testing, can demonstrate relocation of that stored learned function away from the tumour location, allowing total tumour resection without an impact on the patient. How the brain achieves this is not fully understood, but it serves to demonstrate how truly impressive our brains are at learning.

Knowledge of neuroanatomy allows us to think about learning in terms of the structures and processes it involves. Early social learning can be linked to development of tracts of the right hemisphere and of the limbic system (involved in emotional processing). This is then followed by greater importance of the posterior regions of the brain for visual, audio and tactile learning. The frontal lobes are important for planning and evaluation, as well as adaptive behaviour that draws on previous experiences. Higher cognitive functions develop much later during adolescence and depend on the refined development of white matter tracts. With these connecting tracts comes the ability to think and change behaviours. As a brain matures, the brain becomes increasingly interconnected between different neural networks, important for the formation of new memories and the connection of new with previous learning. Considering this anatomy and how learning is linked to our previous learning, experiences, senses and emotional attachments allows us to recognise how the ability to learn varies significantly between individuals.

Metacognition is where the worlds of teaching and neuroscience overlap, with key components from each coming together in collaboration as the processes of learning are considered alongside neurological development and maturity. With brain maturation comes readiness to learn, and this is a vital consideration during the period of our lives when we have the greatest exponential growth – our school years. To a certain extent, this is taken into account by structured school curriculums according to age. However, just as the external appearance of our bodies grows and matures at different rates, the same applies internally to our brains, with different brain functions maturing at differing rates. It is paramount to recognise this as effective learning depends on minimising disparities between teaching instruction and brain maturity.

I find myself thinking about how I learn as I embark on some time in children's brain cancer research as a molecular biologist. Metacognition has proved invaluable as I recognise the way that I learn has changed significantly as an adult. Now is not the time for me to be the rote learner. I need to understand why, how, the practicalities, to visualise, to plan and to challenge. I draw on my ten-year experience of meeting patients with clinical problems, operating on the brain as an organ with its vast and evolving interconnected neural networks, and relate these to the molecular processes I am now learning about. This approach to learning will be completely different to the research scientists I work alongside in the laboratory with no clinical experience. Certainly, metacognition is a life skill, providing a tool to adjust individual learning at any point in our lives according to the unique set of circumstances and experiences that have brought us to that point. As such, there is an importance for it to be taught and adopted at a time when our learning changes the most, arming pupils with the ability to understand and tailor their own individual approach to learning, in turn making learning a more enjoyable and rewarding experience.

'The greatest of all pleasures is the pleasure of learning.' – Aristotle

Ms Louise F. Steele Saukila, MA (Cantab et Oxon), BMBCh (Oxon), MRCS (Eng)

Cancer Research UK Clinical Research Training Fellow at University College London and Neurosurgical Registrar at Great Ormond Street Hospital for Children

Introduction

It's Thursday afternoon. We have spent two weeks learning some critical content and going over exam technique. I have explained, modelled, quizzed, questioned, explored and given feedback. It is now time for a go under timed conditions.

'Any questions? Great. Right, you've got 35 minutes – absolute silence. Off you go.'

> Miss, do we need to write in paragraphs?

> Yes. This is an essay and I have spent two weeks modelling paragraphs with you.

> Miss, what do I do when I get to the bottom of the page?

> Turn the page over.

> Miss, how long do we have?

> There is an enormous timer counting you down on the board.

> Miss, how do I start?

> We did a lesson two days ago on strategies for how to start. We recapped it five minutes ago.

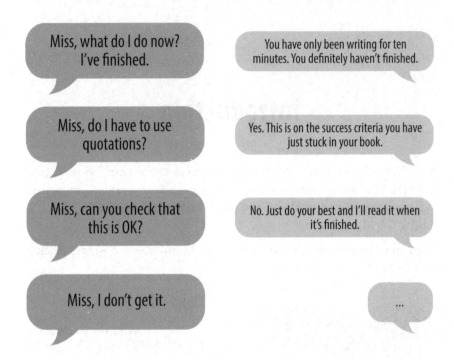

Miss, what do I do now? I've finished.

You have only been writing for ten minutes. You definitely haven't finished.

Miss, do I have to use quotations?

Yes. This is on the success criteria you have just stuck in your book.

Miss, can you check that this is OK?

No. Just do your best and I'll read it when it's finished.

Miss, I don't get it.

...

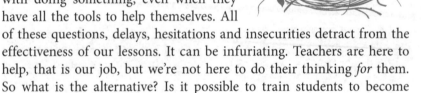

Sound familiar? I've heard this described as 'baby bird syndrome' where students exhibit a strange helplessness when faced with doing something, even when they have all the tools to help themselves. All of these questions, delays, hesitations and insecurities detract from the effectiveness of our lessons. It can be infuriating. Teachers are here to help, that is our job, but we're not here to do their thinking *for* them. So what is the alternative? Is it possible to train students to become independent learners with intrinsic motivation?

We have all taught those students – the ones who just seem to be born with it. Meet Amina.

Amina

- Checked her unit overview before lessons - came ready with questions about key words and ideas.
- Looked at homework tasks, predicted where she would struggle and stayed back to ask questions for clarification. And made notes.
- Made notes, during lessons which she then annotated with further questions for herself.
- Put a pink star on any piece of work where she had improved something, then she would flick back through her book to find them when she attempted new tasks.
- Struggled with tense - kept a laminated grammar reminder in her pencil case until she had memorised its content, and then always checked tenses before handing in a piece of work.
- When she did assessments, she used to write a little note to me at the bottom (I think I have probably missed marks because...).
- Invented songs to help her remember key vocabulary for her essays.

Amina was independent. She was self-motivated and actively aware of herself as a learner. As an EAL learner, she made incredible progress in a short space of time and has continued to do so in higher education. We don't often see many students with this level of innate self-knowledge and drive. Amina was a unicorn. I want a whole school full of unicorns. Metacognition is about exactly this. Making unicorns. Making our students the best possible versions of themselves by training them to work truly independently, constantly pushing for improvement and being intentional in all that they do. So often schools rely on great teachers to drag passive students through their lessons and ensure that they get some qualifications. Imagine how much could be achieved if students were meeting their teachers halfway. Better yet, imagine if it were the students, not the teachers, who were doing the majority of the heavy lifting. A fully engaged, motivated and independent student paired with a phenomenal teacher could achieve anything.

Metacognition: a strange controversy

Metacognition is not new. It has been around for almost 50 years and there is a vast array of research and analysis supporting its effectiveness. It is solid. It builds on a foundation of cognitive science and our understanding of how the most effective learners operate. Many of the core pillars of pedagogy have metacognitive practices and ideas weaved into them: cognitive load theory, formative assessment, generative learning, retrieval practice, modelling. In addition to this, most teachers are already using metacognitive practices – some consciously, some unconsciously. We know instinctively that learners who are independent, motivated and self-aware are more successful.

The EEF toolkit ranks metacognition and self-regulation as the second highest impact strategy of all classroom practices, sitting just behind feedback.

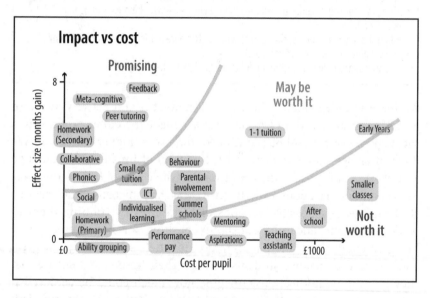

They describe it as 'high impact for very low cost, based on extensive evidence'. That 'extensive evidence' finds that students can make an average of seven months of additional progress per year. It also finds that such strategies can be particularly effective for prior low achieving pupils. Metacognition is highly effective and cheap. So why isn't it ubiquitous in our schools and constantly reviewed and refined in the same way as our feedback policies and assessment frameworks? There are two barriers: politics and implementation.

Politics

Metacognition and self-regulated learning has been the victim of raging politics within the profession. Lumped in with many spurious 'theories' such as learning styles and multiple intelligences (now widely debunked), metacognition has suffered by association and been derided by some as being incompatible with a recent move toward evidence-informed, traditionalist, knowledge-rich curriculum and classroom practice. In 2013, Tom Bennett said: 'Learning to learn: it isn't even a thing. We've been hoaxed... the hipsters are selling snake oil on this one, whether they know it or not.' Bennett sees 'learning to learn' as another initiative based on weak theory, leading to time and resource waste for little return. Metacognition has been wrapped up in various labels (learning to learn, growth mindset) and each of these carries their own baggage. This book does not seek to advocate nor discredit any of these theories. The only aim here is to extrapolate metacognition from its historical baggage and amplify this powerful, evidence-based tool.

I am not interested in the politics of over-simplification and polarisation which are rife in the education sphere. I am interested in what works and what will benefit students and their teachers. Metacognition works. It is as simple as that. No matter what your teacher politics, metacognition can provide a framework to enable your students to learn more effectively and to greatly sustain their development.

Implementation

'Implementing' things in schools is complex and often problematic. I would question any leadership team which seeks to impose top-down initiatives in teaching and learning by diktat. New classroom practice requires a change in behaviours: teacher learning at a profound level. This doesn't happen just because staff have been told to do something on an Inset day. Many teachers only have a vague or partial understanding of what metacognition is. As often happens with sound pedagogical theory, it is either over-simplified or over-complicated and loses its nuance and impact. Metacognition is not a set of non-negotiables. It is not a reflective plenary or an exit ticket. It is not a worksheet or a set of sentence starters. Metacognition is a range of behaviours which are long term and sustained.

To further complicate matters, metacognition is not something which is *done to* students, such as a pop quiz or live modelling. Metacognition is something which students do *themselves*. Anything which requires students to work truly independently is far more difficult to achieve. For it to work, students must be led slowly and assuredly toward independent self-regulation as an ingrained habit. It takes time to train them to do this well and this skill must then be maintained.

Teachers and school leaders must be brave enough to invest the time in doing something meaningful which may not reach fruition straight away. Schools are often quick to adopt new strategies, but also too quick to abandon them. How often have you seen new initiatives fall by the wayside after six months because the impact isn't yet obvious or the strategy needs some improvement? We have to stick with it and invest time in making it work.

In addition, for us to be *metacognitive*, we need a very strong foundational understanding of cognition. Teachers must already understand how learning happens from a cognitive science perspective to optimise that process through metacognitive approaches. Staff CPD is critical and this takes time and patience to do well. It is clear that for metacognition to be implemented successfully it requires a long-term focus. It is not a short-term fix.

Long vs. short-term strategy in schools

One of the great barriers to school improvement is the conflict between culturally imposed time structures versus the reality of how people actually learn. Schools work on very traditional time frames: half-terms, terms, academic years, two-year GCSE specifications. Accountability measures and pressures on results year-on-year have a significant impact on schools. Reputation, inspection, staff retention and recruitment are just a few key areas which can be materially damaged by poor results. The system as we know it traps schools in a 'performity cycle' (Robert-Holmes, 2015) where they become obsessed with short-term outcomes rather than sustainable, long-term growth.

We are operating mostly on yearly cycles, but our students are operating very differently. Seven years in primary school, five years in secondary school, usually two years in further education. If the young people we teach are to go on to professions in law or medicine, for example, they may not be fully qualified until they approach their 30s – some professional training takes even longer than this. Whilst we work on our short-sighted yearly cycles, our students need the long-term view of their at least 14 years in the education system.

Independence is the ultimate goal of education. We are preparing young people to go out into the wider world where they will be flying solo. We must empower them to navigate the many trials and challenges which might come their way. They will have to independently apply things they know and use the skills they have to succeed in new situations. Sometimes these situations might be relatively close to their academic studies in school. They might find themselves in a university lecture hall where they are developing their existing learning and note-taking skills as they continue their journey as students – challenging, yes, but familiar territory. However, they might find themselves in situations which are radically different. They might take on jobs or responsibilities which are entirely new to them. We would hope that our teaching can help prepare them to approach any new, unexpected challenges which come their way.

A metacognitive person approaches new tasks with all the experience and understanding which previous tasks have given them. They don't come to things like a novice, they begin by recognising similarities and differences with things they have seen and done before. They identify what strategies they could use and where they will need to adapt. They monitor their performance during any activity and reflect afterwards. People like this are well equipped to face the challenges which life might throw at them, and this can go beyond the academic and professional spheres. This is the kind of independence we want for our students.

This book will provide clear definitions of the key concepts in metacognition and provide practical guidance to help teachers and school leaders to embed metacognition in their settings. Metacognition can have significant impact on a small scale by an individual teacher and a single class. It also has enormous potential when embedded as a more holistic practice across a school and infiltrates more than just academic learning. We have a duty to see beyond the short-term and educate our young people with ambition and vision which reaches beyond any exam or fixed point. This book is not for people who teach for an exam. This book is for people who teach with their sights set on the horizon, who believe that all students can become the best versions of themselves.

References

Bennett, T. (2013) *Teacher Proof: Why research in education doesn't always mean what it claims, and what you can do about it.* London: Routledge, pp. 160-170.

Roberts-Holmes, G. (2015) 'The 'datafication' of early years pedagogy: 'if the teaching is good, the data should be good and if there's bad teaching, there is bad data", *Journal of Education Policy* 30 (3) pp. 302-315.

Chapter 1
What is metacognition?

Metacognition is a set of behaviours which maximise the potential for and efficacy of learning. Different people have defined it in slightly different ways, but for the purposes of this book I am working with this definition:

> 'A metacognitive learner is one who has knowledge and control over cognitive skills and processes. They understand how learning happens, and they are able to actively and independently apply this understanding to help them learn in the most effective way, and to sustain that learning into the future.'

As you can see, metacognition is a nebulous concept which covers a range of different skills and actions. I am going to divide metacognition into three separate strands, drawing partly from the Education Endowment Foundation (Quigley et al, 2018) and partly from the work of Tova Michalsky (2013):

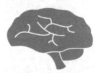

Metacognitive knowledge:	**Metacognitive regulation:**	**Metacognitive motivation:**
knowledge that a learner has about the task at hand, what they know about themselves as a learner, and what learning strategies they know which will help them to complete the task.	the learner's ability to plan, monitor and evaluate their own learning *whilst completing* the task. This is about *actively* applying their metacognitive knowledge in real time.	the extent to which a learner *wants* to perform a task, related closely to their interest in the task and belief in their ability to succeed (self-efficacy).

Task: Completing an essay in timed conditions: *How does Shakespeare present masculinity in the play?*

How did it go last time? Is there anything I need to remember? How do I feel about doing it now? I struggled to start last time – I need to start by rephrasing the question, and use 'DDR' to structure my introduction. I also need to ensure that I am always returning to the question by using the key words or synonyms (e.g. violence, masculinity). Last time I wrote well about context, so I will make sure I do that again. I am feeling apprehensive about this task, but I have to remind myself that this is something I have done before, so I know I am capable of it.

Are there any structures or principles I've been taught which will help? I've been taught to write a plan with my key ideas – choose three parts of the play where masculinity is explored. I will also draw the analysis pyramid to remind myself – sound-word-line-text.

Have I seen or done anything like this before? Yes – I wrote an essay on violence last week. I have written lots of essays and seen lots of models.

What do I already know about this task and the theme? I've learned about masculinity related to different male characters, and I know about Elizabethan ideas of masculinity from previous lessons.

What is the task? Write an essay about masculinity. Essay = introduction, 3+ paragraphs, conclusion.

THROUGHOUT: Student is aware of what they are doing, how they are doing it and how they *feel* about it. They regularly check themselves, identify and correct errors.

AFTERWARDS: How did it go? Could I have approached this another way? How? What will I do next time I face a similar task? How will it be different? How will it be the same? Why?

What errors might I make? What can I do to avoid them? I struggle with spellings of some key context words: *Renaissance, contemporary, patriarchy*. I'll make sure I spend five minutes proof-reading at the end.

This student is doing their work metacognitively. They are going through a series of internalised questions, e.g. 'have I seen or done anything like this before?', and they are using these to identify for themselves what they should do next. They aren't putting their hand up to say, 'Miss, I don't get it.' They are only going to do that if they have exhausted all of their own metacognitive toolkit and still don't have an answer.

The student goes through all three areas of metacognition:

Knowledge: identifying what the task is asking them to do, recalling the things which they have been taught, and deciding which of those things would be most useful to them now. They are reflecting on their own common errors and pre-empting those with a clear strategy. They are remembering how they performed the last time so that they can continue their development, build on successes and address areas of weakness.

Regulation: they are aware of themselves *throughout* the task, they are also able to make corrections as they go and identify trends in their behaviour. Reflection following the task is a way of ensuring that they can put all of these powerful strategies in place again the next time, continuing that upward trajectory.

Motivation: considering how they feel about the task before, during and afterwards. Using strategies to inspire or reassure themselves in order to push through. The student understands that it is natural to feel nervous or lack motivation about a piece of work, but by being *aware* of those feelings they can help themselves to push through and be successful anyway.

Doing metacognition vs. *behaving* metacognitively

As you can see from the example above, a metacognitive learner is highly skilled. This level of knowledge and independence – as with anything else we do in the classroom – takes time. This is not achieved by 'doing' metacognition activities in the classroom. Giving students a reflective plenary every few weeks is not the same as teaching them to be metacognitive learners. Instead, we must see metacognition as a framework around everything else we do.

For example, if someone is teaching a unit of work, they might have roughly the following structure:

Baseline test – activate prior knowledge and inform future lessons	Teach new content: direct instruction, student research and reading	End of unit assessment – gauge student progress and inform needs for future learning
	Teach new skills: teacher modelling, student practice	
	Ongoing spaced and interleaved retrieval of old and new content	
	Ongoing cycle of practice and feedback which informs lessons in the short term	

This follows many of the key pillars of sound teaching practice: direct instruction, reading, activating prior knowledge, retrieval, feedback, independent practice, etc.

With a metacognitive frame, we can take that effective structure and optimise it:

Look at a *brief* topic overview: How do you feel about this topic? Does it interest you? What can you do to ensure that you are making the most of studying it?

REFLECTION: How do I do in this test? What do I already know about this topic? What *don't* I already know? How can I ensure that I focus on this content as we go through this unit?

Baseline test – activate prior knowledge and inform future lessons

QUESTIONS alongside new learning: What is this about? What do I already know about this? What strategies can I use to help me learn? (note-taking, reading strategies, etc.)

REFLECTION after practising skill or retrieval: Have I improved? How? Will I change my approach next time? How?

Teach new content: direct instruction, student research and reading

Teach new skills: teacher modelling, student practice

Ongoing spaced and interleaved retrieval of old and new content

Ongoing cycle of practice and feedback which informs lessons in the short term

PREDICT: How do I think the assessment will go? How confident do I feel? What mistakes am I likely to make? What can I do to prevent those from happening! What have I done successfully during this unit? How can I make sure I sustain that success?

End of unit assessment – gauge student progress and inform needs for future learning

REFLECTION after the assessment: How did the assessment go? What were my successes and failures? Why? How do the knowledge and skills from this topic link to the next one? What should I take forward into my future learning?

QUESTIONS throughout the process: What <u>trends</u> can I identify in my work? What do I tend to do well? Why? What are my <u>common errors</u>? What can I do about them? Can I approach problems in different ways? What <u>strategies</u> have I been taught which will help me? How do I feel about this topic and the skills I am trying to develop? What can I do to help <u>motivate</u> myself?

This is the same unit of work structure but with a metacognitive frame. The questions and prompts in this framework serve to optimise the unit of work and support students to be self-aware and reflective in their learning. I see this metacognitive framework as a guard against passivity. Students can't float through their lessons expecting to learn things by simple exposure to a teacher if they are regularly engaging in metacognitive questions which force them to identify their strengths, weaknesses, successes, failures and motivation whilst also strategically planning for future learning. Nothing is passive. Everything they do is deliberate and purposeful. The metacognitive classroom is an intentional classroom.

A teacher who uses metacognitive approaches as a framework for their teaching is able to train their students over time to *behave* metacognitively. By giving explicit, scaffolded support in the first instance and gradually removing the stabilisers, we can make baby birds into unicorns.

References

Michalsky, T. (2013) 'Integrating Skills and Wills Instruction in Self-Regulated Science Text Reading for Secondary Students', *International Journal of Science Education* 35 (11) pp. 1846-1873.

Quigley, A., Muijs, D. and Stringer, E. (2018) *Metacognition and Self Regulated Learning: Guidance Report.* Education Endowment Foundation. Retrieved from: www.bit.ly/3u6zual

Chapter 2

The classroom: practical ways to teach metacognitively

'There is an abundance of compelling research evidence to suggest that teaching pupils in ways that engage and develop metacognitive and self-regulatory processing leads to demonstrable, statistically significant gains across a range of pupil outcomes.'

Dr James Mannion and Kate McAllister (2020)

I have found that one of the greatest challenges in leading teaching and learning is overcoming the tendency we have in schools to grab hold of the immediate, easy thing. It is easy to say, 'here is a checklist of things you must do in the classroom – these are the ingredients of a good lesson'. Easy but not effective in the long term. It doesn't enable teachers to develop, doesn't recognise the critical differences between subject disciplines, and is often too focused on 'initiatives' and 'activities' without really engaging with the long-term complexity of the learning process. There is nothing wrong with encouraging teachers to plan effective activities in their lessons, but our focus should be less on individual tasks and more on sustained and interconnected behaviours. For example, I want staff in my school to use metacognitive strategies effectively. If I focus on activities alone, I might show them some different ways they can 'do' metacognition: reflective plenary, metacognitive talk, modelling. I might say: please use these activities regularly in your lessons to develop student metacognitive skill.

This would probably work to an extent – teachers would be using pretty effective strategies that students would likely benefit from.

What happens though when those activities aren't appropriate for the type of knowledge or skill which is being taught in a particular topic? What happens when teachers need to be flexible and responsive in the classroom? I have given them some activities, but I haven't given them the tools they need to respond in the moment to changes in student need. Their understanding of metacognition is based solely on activities, rather than on their behaviours as a teacher in the classroom and student behaviours as metacognitive learners. We need to move from 'I'm using some metacognition in my lessons' or 'I did some metacognition in maths' to '**I teach metacognitively**' and '**I learn metacognitively**'.

Throughout this chapter, you will find a range of classroom strategies which you can use as a foundation for changing behaviours. They are simple, flexible ideas which build upon the core principles of effective teaching.

1. How do you train students to be metacognitive?
2. Modelling
3. Metacognitive talk
4. Challenge
5. Feedback
6. Vocabulary
7. Schemas
8. Case studies

1. How do you train students to be metacognitive?

There are many different structures in existence for teaching metacognition. Perhaps the most well-known is 'plan, monitor, evaluate' where students plan a strategy, monitor their performance during the task, and then evaluate its success. This works in a cycle and students are able to then apply their evaluation to the planning of their next task, as illustrated in the following graphic by the Education Endowment Foundation (2018).

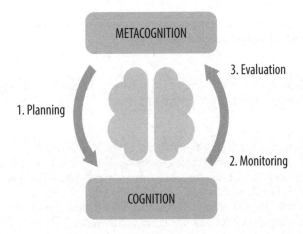

This is an effective approach but I prefer to use **comprehension, connection, strategy** and **reflection**, based on the work of Tova Michalsky (2013).

Put simply this approach teaches students to:

- identify what they understand about the task/topic/information (COMPREHENSION).
- make links between this task/topic/information and things they have seen before (CONNECTION).
- identify the best approach they can use to complete the task (STRATEGY).
- evaluate how successful their approach was and how they felt about it (REFLECTION).

I prefer this approach because it is more closely aligned with what we know about how the brain learns, as shown in the following graphic.

1. The brain encounters new information via sensory stimulus *e.g. I see some information on a 16th century map of Europe in a history lesson.*

2. The brain breaks up the new information and **sorts it into different areas** *(this might relate to image and shape, language, concept, number, etc.).*

3. The brain searches for **recognisable similarities** to knowledge which it already has and makes links. The more knowledge the brain already has, the more links it can make, the more powerful the learning. This is the brain building neural networks. *e.g. I've seen a map of Europe before. I know how maps work - these lines are borders, this is the sea, these are cities etc. I know things about France. I know what people might have looked like during this period of time. I know that Shakespeare was from this period...*

4. Over time with new experiences, the brain continues to develop these networks. Every new encounter sees the brain updating and reprogramming itself – memory is fluid: knowledge which is engaged with repeatedly and adapted by new connections is made stronger. *E.g. I encounter a newer map of Europe which has some different country names. I learn about Mount Vesuvius in geography and I am able to link this knowledge to my existing mental map of Europe.*

The comprehension, connection and strategy elements of Michalsky's approach are very much in concert with how we learn. These cognitive processes also explain to us why repetition and recall works: we strengthen neural pathways every time we engage with a piece of knowledge. This doesn't just work for knowledge but for behaviours too. When you practise a skill, your neural pathways associated with that skill are strengthened and the task becomes easier. Over time, those actions might become automated and unconscious. If students are regularly practising metacognitive skills, such as making explicit connections between new and prior learning, and independently selecting strategies to succeed in tasks, these skills will eventually become second nature to them.

How do you train students to be metacognitive? It all starts with questioning. Questioning is the most powerful tool we have in the classroom. We can pose questions to explore, to probe, to challenge, to push, to give feedback, to change direction, to test, to encourage.

Our aim in metacognition is to train students to ask *themselves* a series of internal questions when they are working. I use knowledge, regulation and motivation to structure my questioning in the following way:

KNOWLEDGE

Comprehension What is this task/event/information about? What do I understand about it? What is it asking me to do?

Connection What do I already know about this? Have I seen anything like this before? What are the similarities and differences between this and other things in my past experiences?

Strategy Do I know any strategies which would be appropriate for this task/problem? Which strategy would be the most helpful to me now?

REGULATION

Strategy Have I used this strategy before? Was it successful? Why? How can I ensure that I am successful this time?

During the task How is this going? What are my common errors in tasks like this? How can I avoid making those? What am I finding difficult right now? Why? What am I doing well? How do I know?

Reflection after the task Does my finished work look successful? Does it make sense? How do I know? Could I have approached this in a different way? Is this work an improvement on things I have done in the past? How?

MOTIVATION

During the task How do I feel about the work? Am I motivated to complete this task to a high standard? What can I do to improve my motivation level right now?

Reflection after the task How did my motivation level affect my performance in that task? What emotions did I experience during the task? Why? How can I motivate myself in a different way in the future? Explain.

These questions form the basis of everything I do in metacognition.

When I'm at the very start of training my students to think, talk, act and write metacognitively, I use sentence stems to help scaffold their thought processes. Think of these as flexible supports which can be varied according to need until students no longer require them.

Beginner reflection after a task

Using these sentence stems, students can begin to think about how they found a task or lesson, and how they can take that experience and use it to plan for improving next time.

Beginner pre-mortem

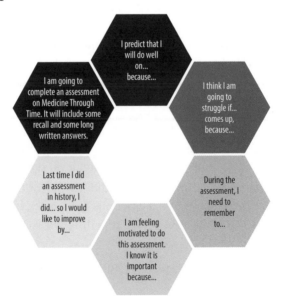

Students use the stems to consider what an upcoming assessment might look like, how they might perform, and how they can ensure they do their best. This enables them to create a strategy based on their observations of themselves and understanding of what is coming.

Focused reflection on exam skills

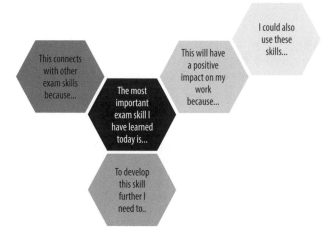

Students use these to identify where they learn and develop exam skills. They can connect those skills to other topics and recognise how they fit in to the bigger picture.

Reflection on knowledge

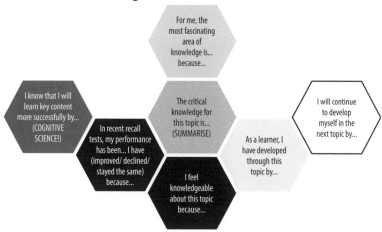

Students use their understanding of how recall aids long-term knowledge retention. They reflect on their confidence level on a topic, identify how they have improved and link this to their knowledge of themselves as a learner. They consider their breadth of knowledge and are able to summarise and make judgements about the topic. They can see how their skills as a learner is developing and can plan to make improvements for the future.

I like hexagons but you can use any visual you like. The key idea is that students are given a step-by-step approach to metacognitive thinking and writing in the early stages of their skill development. They use the sentence starter in each hexagon – starting with the black hexagon but then in any order they like – to write a developed reflection. Hexagons can be arranged in any pattern you like and adapted for any subject, topic or focus, or to meet specific needs of students. They are totally flexible and can be used in countless configurations. Students might also use blank hexagons to develop their own stages towards metacognition. This is just scaffolding. Over time, I vary and diminish the support so that students are eventually able to reflect far more independently and with fewer prompts.

I also use very simple grids to structure metacognitive work when I don't want students to do extended writing. Grids are great because they don't need to be a prepared resource and students can easily draw these into an exercise book. I'm a big fan of anything which I can do without having planned it in advance because it frees me up to be more responsive and flexible in my teaching.

Task:

Comprehension (What is the task asking you to do?)	Connection (Have you ever done or seen anything like this before? How is this similar or different?)
Strategy (Based on past experience, what is the best approach for you to use for this task?)	Reflection (How did it go? How did you feel about it? What will you change for next time?)

Example of one from an RE class:

Task: Explain two Muslim teachings about Prophet Muhammad (PBUH)

Comprehension (What is the task asking you to do?)	Connection (Have you ever done or seen anything like this before? How is this similar or different?)
• 'explain' — key word, give information and expand on it • 'two' — must cover two different teachings • Write in paragraphs — one paragraph for each teaching • Mark scheme: refer to scripture, refer to impact on Muslim daily life	• Exam question last week — on Christianity but similar structure and same mark scheme • We have done recall tests on Islamic teachings • I have done research tasks on the life of Prophet Muhammad • I have seen two model answers for this kind of question and we annotated them • This question structure will be on all my RE exam papers for different topics
Strategy (Based on past experience, what is the best approach for you to use for this task?)	Reflection (How did it go? How did you feel about it? What will you change for next time?)
• Last week on the Christianity question I forgot to refer to the Bible, so I lost half the marks. I need to remember to use at least 2 references to Islamic scripture • Use simple sentence structure, like Miss used in the model answer: 'One key Muslim teaching about Muhammad is...' • 4 minutes per paragraph • Double check key spellings at the end (make sure you are always spelling Muhammad correctly and consistently)	• I have improved by 3 marks since last time — better use of scripture • I used my time better and stuck to 4 mins per paragraph, but felt stressed by the end. I need to remind myself to stay calm — this isn't the most important type of question so I need to move on to the 12 mark essay and not be so obsessed by little details!

2. Modelling

'Revealing the thought processes of an expert learner.' (Quigley et al, 2018)

A teacher models by physically doing an activity in front of students. For example, a PE teacher might model to their students how to stand, place their feet, turn their body and hold a cricket bat correctly. This becomes more powerful when the teacher verbalises their thought processes, e.g. 'I am placing my back foot on the crease like this, because it gives me the distance to be able to step back or forwards in response to the ball when it is released. I'm going to make a mark on the crease in front of me in line with the middle wicket so that I don't have to look at it. I'm going to shift my stance slightly now because I'm not fully balanced.'

This process of thinking out loud is absolutely critical because it removes the mystery. Learning new things is incredibly difficult and it is important to be explicit about what things look like: what an expert writer, musician, artist, runner, baker, reader, biologist or geographer looks like. It's also important to explicitly model the metacognitive process, e.g. 'Last time I swung at the ball, I... so this time I'm going to...' or 'that wasn't very successful, so I'm going to try... and it's important that I remember to...'. Virtually everything we teach can be explicitly modelled. If this PE teacher follows the 'knowledge, regulation, motivation' question structure, asking those questions of themself as they model, they can show students not just what a successful cricketer looks like but what a metacognitive learner looks like.

Top tips for metacognitive modelling:

I, We, You

Move in stages from teacher led work to students working independently.

I: Start by explicitly modelling for students yourself.

> 'I am doing this because...'
> 'I am selecting this word because...'
> 'I am looking for these elements because...'

...and model your metacognitive process as the expert learner:

'I know that I tend to... so I'm going to make sure that I...'
'Last time I did this I forgot... so I'm going to...'
'I've noticed that I'm missing... so I need to...'
'I'm noticing that this is drifting away from the question, so I need to...'
'I feel anxious about... so I'm trying to remind myself that...'

We: Then move into co-creating work with students. You partially model as above, but invite contributions from the students and prompt them to bring their metacognitive knowledge and regulation into that activity with them.

'What have we learned which would help us to start?'
'Can anyone give us an opening phrase?'
'Great, why is that an effective way to start?'
'How exactly should I phrase that?'
'Why did you choose X word instead of X word?'
'What are some of the common mistakes we might make when we are doing this?'
'What could we do while we write to avoid those mistakes?'
'Can anyone see a problem with this line? What could we improve? Why is that more effective?'

You: Students complete work independently using all the principles you have taught them. By this point, they should have a really firm understanding of what a successful piece of work looks like, be able to explain the optimal process for completing it, and identify in themselves the key things which they need to remember in order to be successful. In order to support students initially, you could do the following things:

- Provide metacognitive prompt questions (selecting some from the knowledge, regulation, motivation list).

- Ask students to write down three key things they need to remember based on their feedback from previous work.

- Give students core content they might need (such as key vocabulary, definitions or dates), if you think appropriate.

The critical point with 'I, We, You' is that the learning process is messy and complex. It isn't sufficient for us to simply say, this is 'what a good one looks like', and then expect students to be able to produce something of quality immediately. Modelling takes far more than just one or two examples because powerful learning takes repetition, variation and depth. By starting with teacher modelling and then slowly taking away the stabilisers, students have the opportunity to develop slowly toward independence.

Modelling the work review

We very often show students how to create a successful piece of work but we don't always show them how to quality assure it when they have finished. Students sometimes hand work in which is very obviously incorrect or clearly missing a key ingredient. They have come to the end and are no longer interested in regulating themselves because they see it as 'finished'. Maths teachers will be painfully aware of this – students handing in work where a small but significant error has been made, a slip of a decimal place, a division instead of a multiplication, a positive instead of a negative number, a calculator mistake, and suddenly the student is producing an incorrect answer even though they understand the topic and process perfectly well. It is important to model to students that they check their work afterwards using metacognitive questions like, 'does my solution make sense?'

For example, a simple maths problem might say:

There are twice as many girls in the class as boys. If there are 9 boys, how many girls are there?

This seems very easy, but if a student misreads and divides instead of multiplying, they might put an answer of 4.5.

Asking themselves, 'does my solution make sense?' helps them to identify their error, 'no, you can't have four and a half girls. I must have made a mistake.'

Most of what we do in the classroom is far more complex than this. We need them to be able to review substantial pieces of work in a meaningful way, and it will take time for them to develop this skill. As with everything else, using question prompts is the best strategy:

Does this make sense?
Does this fit the brief? Does this answer the question?

Does this match the success criteria I have been given?

Have I checked my work for my personal common errors?

Am I satisfied that this is the best I can do right now?

Are there any elements of my work I am uncertain about or have questions about?

I find it very useful to get students to consider key questions like this before handing in their work. You might start training them in this method by using talking partners at first. Get students in pairs and have them ask each other these questions about their work.

1. Students complete their work.

2. They use the prompt questions to review their work.

3. They have a conversation with their partner where they discuss those questions and any changes they think they should make.

4. They make the necessary changes.

5. They write a short reflection to make those changes explicit:
   'I identified X error(s) in my first draft, so have made improvements by...'
   'I noticed that I had forgotten to include... so I have added this...'
   'These changes have improved my work by...'
   'Next time I'm going to ensure that I...'

I also often ask students to review their work and write any remaining questions or uncertainties in the margin where appropriate. Students ask themselves: What do I still need to know? What knowledge would have made this work even better?

They might write questions in the margin such as:

'Is this the right way to use this word?'

'Could I have used a more appropriate quotation?'

'Is there another Shakespeare play where something similar to this happens?'

'What did you say last week about this, Miss?'

By identifying these questions for themselves, they are acknowledging the work they still need to do. They are also explicitly saying that, even though they are handing in this piece of work, it's still really a work in progress.

Take the long view

All modelling needs to form part of the long view of education. It is a tool which supports us to build up student skill slowly. For example, if I were teaching students how to write an analytical essay, I wouldn't just model a whole essay straight away. I would build up each element in detail. For example:

- Model reading an essay question: key words, identifying what the task is asking us to do.
- Model the essay planning process.
- Model writing an introductory paragraph.
- Model writing a body paragraph.
- Model word choices: how analytical verbs, abstract nouns and adjectival phrases fit into an opening statement, for example.
- Model sentence structures and key phrases.
- Model ways to link ideas together.
- Model ways to introduce key content.
- Model writing a conclusion paragraph.
- Model how to review the essay before handing it in.
- Model how to re-draft the essay after feedback.

All complex skills which we teach can be broken down into these smaller parts and taught slowly like this.

A **dance** teacher might take time modelling each individual movement before linking them together to form a routine.

A **history** teacher might model the key stages in source analysis: skimming, identifying perspectives, linking to existing knowledge, making comparisons, assessing reliability and then the writing process.

A **food technology** teacher might model the key skills required for baking: reading a recipe, weighing and measuring ingredients, using equipment, mixing, folding, rubbing-in, etc., before linking these elements together and making scones.

Alongside all of these smaller chunks of modelling, we continue to combine disciplinary knowledge with metacognitive knowledge, and thus move towards greater independence in our students.

3. Metacognitive talk

Lev Vygotsky viewed speech and social interaction as playing a fundamental role in the learning process. He posited that when humans learn, their linguistic abilities enable them to give meaning to the things which they perceive. The cognitive process is not simply about seeing and understanding something. It involves the use of language and culture as a framework through which we impose meaning on the world around us:

> 'A special feature of human perception ... is the perception of real objects ... I do not see the world simply in color and shape but also as a world with sense and meaning. I do not merely see something round and black with two hands; I see a clock ...' (Vygotsky, 1978).

Vygotsky argued that learning is actively constructed by learners, not simply because they encounter a shape or colour or sound but because they use language to create meaning. Critically, that use of language is a social experience and therefore learning is co-created between people through talk. Put simply, Vygotsky argued that a critical part of the learning process is social interaction between a student and an external person (usually a teacher), and learners gradually move away from the need for that social guidance towards independence.

We can apply this to metacognition. According to Vygotsky's theory of verbal self-regulation, students move from external talk and guidance, to individual self-talk, to internal self-talk. In other words, they go from a teacher talking them through something, to becoming completely independent. He said that (Vygotsky, 1978):

> 'Every function in the child's cultural development appears twice: first, on the social level and, later on, on the individual level; first, between people (interpsychological) and then inside the child (intrapsychological). This applies equally to voluntary attention, to logical memory, and to the formation of concepts. All the higher functions originate as actual relationships between individuals.'

Metacognitive self-talk: from guided to independent practice

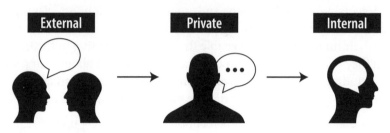

External	Private	Internal
Student actions are directed by an external agent, such as a teacher or a peer.	Students internalise the prompts of the external agent and speak <u>out loud</u> to themselves.	Student self-talk becomes <u>silent</u> and internal.
e.g. Teacher modelling their thought process whilst completing a task: *I am choosing to use this pencil because... I am keeping my right hand relaxed and resting my left hand on the paper here. This will mean that I can draw more freely.*	*e.g.* Student talking to themselves using learned prompts: *I am going to focus on directional cross-hatching during this sketch – I need to try to stay focused so that my work at the end is the same quality as my work at the start, and the lines stay close together. I am going to stop and quality check my work every five minutes so that I can be sure I am being consistent.*	*Students independently consider and explore metacognitive questions as part of their natural thinking process*
Teacher asking prompting questions to support learner reflection: *How did you feel during that activity? How successful is your cross-hatching? Have you used directional lines? Does it look like a round object? How could you improve next time?*		

In the classroom, we can promote this journey from guided to independent talk by doing the following things:

External

- Explicitly speaking out loud our thought process when we model tasks in front of students.

- Giving prompts to students to support them to develop their metacognitive knowledge, regulation and motivation during group discussion, or one-to-one conversations in the classroom.

- Using talking partners and getting students to prompt and question each other.

- Asking students to use metacognitive question prompts in a discussion with somebody at home as part of home learning.

Private

- Giving students written prompts and asking them to speak to themselves out loud before, during and after a piece of work. Depending on your class, this might be something you can do in a lesson where students just focus on their own self-talk, though this may not be appropriate in all situations. Students can use written prompts to talk out loud as part of home learning.

- Get students to model their own 'talk out loud' process for the rest of the class, e.g. rather than *teacher* modelling, get a *student* to show their work (under a visualiser, or in some other way) and talk the class through how this was achieved. Once students are comfortable with this, you might move to the more challenging task of a student *live* modelling in front of the class, though this is advanced metacognitive work!

- As a homework task, ask students to record themselves reflecting on a piece of work or learning they have completed. You might give them four or five questions and ask them to record themselves talking for two minutes, expanding on the 'why' and 'how'.

Internal

At this point, students are able to apply metacognitive principles independently and are actively *thinking* through the kinds of questions and prompts which have previously been spoken to them and *by* them. When I have students who are this well trained, I like to include recall questions about their metacognitive knowledge as part of their normal retrieval practice. For example, we might be doing a recall quiz with 20 questions. Most of the questions would be subject-specific content we had been covering (e.g. the Renaissance period, WW1 poetry, grammar rules) but a couple of the questions would be things like:

- What is the best strategy you know for proofreading? When was the last time you used it? Would you change it in any way?

- If I asked you to complete a timed written assessment on this topic now, how would you feel about it? Why? What could you do to motivate yourself?

Bodrova (2006) has explained the link between Vygotsky's theory and the development of students:

> 'For Vygotsky, self-regulation is not a single trait or even a combination of traits but rather a critical development signalling emergence of uniquely human set of competencies "higher mental functions". While not using the word "self-regulation" to describe higher mental functions, Vygotsky described them though as deliberate, intentional, or volitional behaviors, as something that humans have control of. Acquiring higher mental functions allows children to make a critical transition from being "slaves to the environment" to becoming "masters of their own behavior". This process requires children to master specific cultural tools – including language and other symbolic systems – which they can use to gain control over their physical, emotional, and cognitive functioning.'

It is through the effective use of language in the classroom that we empower students to 'gain control' over the cognitive process.

4. Challenge

There is no point in asking a student to reflect metacognitively on what is and is not working for them if there is no challenge to interrogate. As educators, we know that challenge is critical to the learning process; learning is more effective when students experience struggle in a positive way. What we often aren't aware of is the role of challenge as a vital part of the mechanical process of learning. Essentially, if the brain finds something difficult or encounters failure, it grants it personal significance. If we give students work which is highly challenging, they are more likely to transfer information to long-term memory (Brown, Roediger, Mcdaniel, 2014).

High challenge = *better learning*

Important things to consider:
- Challenge must be appropriate. This is not about pushing students so hard that they can't cope. Work should be pitched so that students experience a healthy amount of struggle, but that success is also within their reach.

- What one person finds challenging is different to another. It is important that students are able to identify what is challenging for them and that they are empowered to ask for it. **Metacognitive learners know how the work feels and can identify when something is not pitched appropriately for them.**

- If students understand the cognitive science sitting behind challenge in the classroom, they are more likely to engage and welcome it. **Metacognitive learners are empowered by knowledge about the learning process.**

Zones: comfort – challenge – panic

One way to get students to engage with challenge in a meaningful way is to get them to reflect metacognitively on various tasks you might give them and identify how challenging they find each one. This diagram uses the idea of three different zones:

Comfort zone: tasks in this zone are easy, sometimes boring, and students feel very comfortable with their knowledge and skill level. Completing tasks in this zone will not stretch the student as a learner.

Challenge zone: sometimes called the 'Goldilocks' zone, tasks in this category provide the right level of challenge. They represent a healthy struggle and, though students might find things difficult, they can see that effort will bring results.

Panic zone: tasks here are pitched too high or evoke a negative reaction in students because they are anxious about a deficit in skill or knowledge. This might be an area where they feel that they have missed learning, or don't understand the basics and therefore lack confidence.

It is important to acknowledge that an adolescent brain which is anxious about something is far less likely to embed information in long-term memory. In other words, students in the panic zone are not learning. We want our students to be in the challenge 'sweet spot' as much as possible and, though it is impossible to get *every* student in that range for *every* minute of *every* lesson, there are things we can do to increase our chances.

I get students to use the following template to identify where their optimal levels of challenge lie.

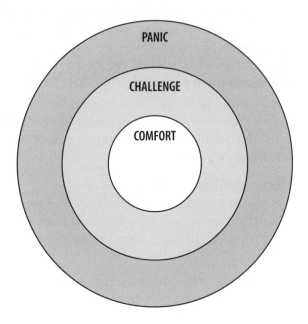

Process:
1. Students are given this template, plus a list of common activities or topics which I regularly set in lessons.
2. Students then place these activities and topics into the appropriate circle.
3. I ask students to look at the items in the 'comfort' and 'panic' zones and annotate each one, explaining why they feel that way.

Example using a list of tasks and knowledge from a SOW on speech writing

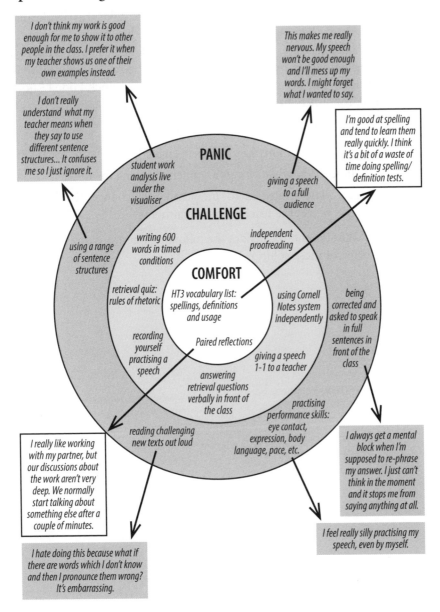

This student has attempted to explain why some of these items are in the 'comfort' or 'panic' zones.

The final stage in this process would then be to take this work and expand on how these tasks, skills and knowledge might be moved into the challenge zone. For example, the student has said, '**reading challenging new texts out loud**' is in the 'panic' zone, explaining that they 'hate doing this because what if there are words which I don't know and then I pronounce them wrong? It's embarrassing.'

I want to use this insight to explore ways in which:

1. I can plan better, more appropriately challenging lessons for them.
2. *they* can identify when things are pitched wrong for them.
3. *they* can plan strategies to independently change the level of challenge, or ask the teacher for adjustments.

I would ask the student to consider the following questions and we might work out some of these solutions:

What could I (the teacher) do differently to support you in reading new texts out loud?	Give me the passage to read beforehand so that it's not completely new. Let me look at it overnight. Or pre-teach some of the vocabulary first using 'I say, you say' so that the whole class practices some new vocabulary and pronunciations before anyone is asked to read out loud.
Have you ever had success in doing this in other subjects? What was different?	I've done this in drama before with play scripts, but it has felt easier because it was as a character and everyone was practising it at the same time so it was OK. **Teacher reflection:** Perhaps if we approach reading new texts out loud as a 'rehearsal' or 'practice' performance, students might feel less pressure?
Break the problem down – is it about confidence with new words, or is it about your anxiety of 'performing' in front of other people?	It's not knowing how to pronounce new words and being worried that people will laugh if I say it wrong. I don't want people to laugh at me. **Teacher reflection:** Psychological safety needs to be a priority in my classroom.
How do you know when you are feeling anxious or overwhelmed by something during a lesson? Are there any warning signs for you?	I find it difficult to think — I get stressed and can't get my words out properly.
What can you do *during* a lesson if you are asked to do something you are uncomfortable with? What could you do *after* that lesson?	I could tell the teacher? And talk about it afterwards? **Teacher reflection:** Give students the tools to politely say, 'please can you ask someone else,' at moments when they are genuinely panicking. This doesn't mean they are off the hook – they can do something similar in a future lesson, but we might approach it differently following a 1-1 conversation.
What skills could we develop which will help you to tackle new texts better in the future?	I could ask for some practice extracts which I can read out loud for homework.

This might seem like a rather lengthy and over-complicated process but it is about giving students the tools they need to be actively engaged in how they learn. As I said in the introduction, we can't do their thinking for them. They must bring their brain to the table and get the most out of their education. With the best will in the world, a teacher cannot possibly work through all the difficulties and anxieties students might have about their work. We also cannot sense every moment when a student is bored, coasting or not feeling intellectually stimulated. If students have the tools to notice these things in themselves, they can *help* themselves.

Challenge and motivation

Challenge is intrinsically linked to self-efficacy and motivation. If we have a high-challenge classroom, we need to have students who are motivated to accept that challenge. Students who explicitly consider levels of challenge and their impact on their own motivation are more likely to be able to manage and be resilient in the face of the difficult skills and tasks in our classrooms.

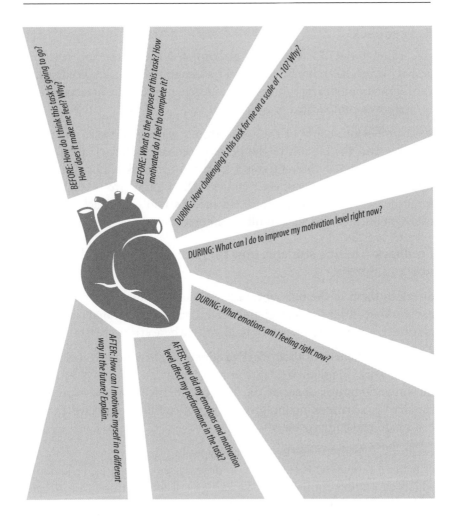

BEFORE: How do I think this task is going to go? How does it make me feel? Why?

BEFORE: What is the purpose of this task? How motivated do I feel to complete it?

DURING: How challenging is this task for me on a scale of 1–10? Why?

DURING: What can I do to improve my motivation level right now?

DURING: What emotions am I feeling right now?

AFTER: How can I motivate myself in a different way in the future? Explain.

AFTER: How did my emotions and motivation level affect my performance in the task?

This is one way for students to work through factors affecting their motivation before, during and after a task. I tend to use this to support students to be metacognitive during timed assessments or more substantial pieces of work where they are completing things mostly independently. Prompts like this enable them to monitor how they are feeling and recognise that having negative emotions about work, or lacking motivation, is completely normal and the best learners have coping strategies to overcome those feelings when they need to get things done.

5. Feedback

According to the EEF (Quigley et al, 2018), feedback is the only teaching activity which has more impact than metacognitive practice. Feedback is the foundation of everything we do as teachers and, like metacognition, is often over-complicated or over-simplified.

As a profession, many of the worst things we have done to ourselves have been in the pursuit of the perfect feedback policy. Triple impact marking using 14 different colours; verbal feedback stamps to prove that we speak to our students; endless 'DIRT tasks' from teachers on a murderous workload treadmill. In many schools, feedback has been over-complicated and, as a result, we have lost its simple power.

Feedback = telling students how they are doing so that they know how to improve

Speak to them in the moment: provide subtle adjustments to how they are working; guide them by giving a steer; reassure them that something is correct; ask probing questions to identify where errors are being made.

Give an assessment of their work product: identify successful elements of their work; highlight areas for improvement; suggest ways in which they might improve; illustrate the difference between their work and the standard you are looking for; give a range of common errors which they can use to make improvements.

Feedback, like anything else done really well in the classroom, isn't a set of printed resources. Feedback is an organic set of teaching *behaviours* which we exhibit consistently. We can give feedback through a simple nod of the head. On the other end of the scale, it can be as complex and specific as numerous comments in the margins of a practice exam, followed by some structured tasks for making improvements. We need the entire spectrum of feedback in our classrooms.

Feedback and metacognition are inextricably linked. Timely, effective feedback enables students to accurately judge the effectiveness of their learning and apply metacognitive principles to their work moving forward. For example, if a student receives feedback in their chemistry lesson that they have misunderstood a key concept, they can plan to rectify this and monitor their progress in this area in future learning. If a student receives feedback in their music lesson that they inadvertently sped up the beat during a performance so that things were too fast by the end, they can metacognitively plan to self-regulate next time. They can decide to practise with a metronome and attempt to be mindful of timing and listen closely to the tempo of their peers during their next performance.

Feedback in these situations was critical, because the students may not have identified these areas for improvement by themselves. Teachers are the expert guides and feedback is our greatest tool. For feedback to have maximum impact, we need students to be metacognitive: taking feedback on board, internalising it and improving future performance.

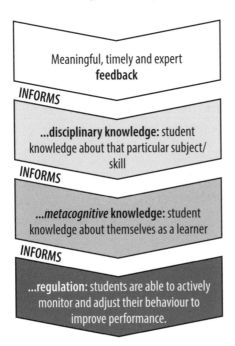

Ways to blend feedback and metacognition

Make it a consistent part of your practice that a key part of any feedback is student reflection. Students should always be guided to consider: what went well, what did not go well, why and what they should do to improve.

This can be as simple as putting these prompt questions onto a whole-class feedback sheet or writing them on the board after a quiz. It doesn't need a fancy resource – it's just about consistent reflective behaviours which allow students to evaluate their performance and move forward.

For those times when we would like to elevate this reflection following feedback, here are some other strategies which I use:

Exam wrappers

An exam wrapper is a set of planning and reflection questions which students complete before and after an assessment. You can add lots of other elements to a wrapper, but the basic idea is very simple.

Before the assessment:

When did you start preparing for this assessment? *(e.g. I have revised regularly all year; I didn't prepare at all...)*			
What did you do to prepare? Circle all that apply:			
Self-quizzing	Created notes summaries	Completed online quizzes	Memorised key content
Studied with a friend or family member	Created flashcards from memory	Other:	
Do you think this has been helpful? How?			

How confident do you feel about this assessment? Why?	
How motivated do you feel? How can you motivate yourself to do your best?	

After the assessment:

What types of questions were the most challenging?	
Type of question	Why did I find this challenging?
e.g. Drawing graphs	

In this assessment I got...

This is an improvement on/the same as/not as good as my last assessment because...

The biggest difference this time was...

 REGULATION: Next time I am going to do better by...

 MOTIVATION: Next time I am going to motivate myself better by...

 My teacher can help me in future by...

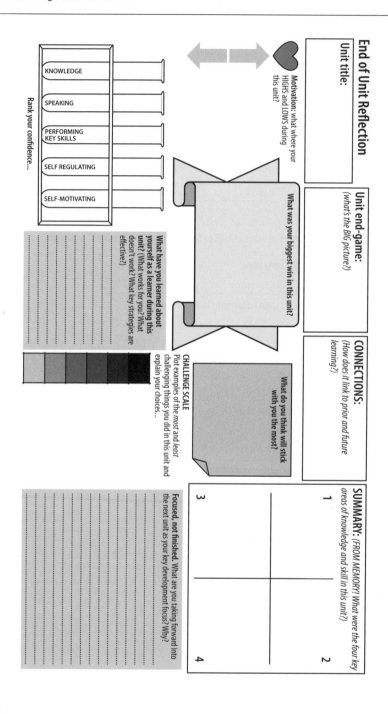

End of Unit Reflection

Unit title:

Motivation: what where your HIGHS and LOWS during this unit?

KNOWLEDGE

SPEAKING

PERFORMING KEY SKILLS

SELF REGULATING

SELF-MOTIVATING

Rank your confidence...

Unit end-game:
(what's the BIG picture?)

What was your biggest win in this unit?

What have you learned about yourself as a learner during this unit? (What works for you? What doesn't work? What key strategies are effective?)

CHALLENGE SCALE
Plot examples of the *most* and *least* challenging things you did in this unit and explain your choices...

CONNECTIONS:
(How does it link to prior and future learning?)

What do you think will stick with you the most?

SUMMARY: *(FROM MEMORY! What were the four key areas of knowledge and skill in this unit?)*

1

2

3

4

Focused, not finished. What are you taking forward into the next unit as your key development focus? Why?

58

I use this end of unit reflection resource to get students to consider their learning over the course of a whole unit of work. It asks them to look back over the subject knowledge and skills they have learned, but also links this with their progress in self-regulation and self-motivation as learners. I've used many versions of this, and put different boxes and prompts in according to what is the most appropriate for the unit and group at hand. The final box is entitled **'Focused, not finished'**. I love this as a statement, it comes from American talk show host Chris Hogan and – while I'm not endorsing everything he says – this phrase is a great mantra for students who are on a long-term school career. They might come to the end of a unit or finish an assessment, but that doesn't mean they are finished. There are things to carry forward and ways to continue to grow. The metacognitive process creates more self-aware learners who recognise their own continuous development.

Sliding scale success criteria

Success criteria	**Predict:** How well will you do?	**Regulate:** How will you be successful?
▢		
▢		
▢		
▢		
▢		
▢		

In the left-hand column, the success criteria for the task at hand give students a clear sense of what they are being asked to do. You can fill this in for them beforehand, or you could get students to look at the task and use their metacognitive knowledge to create a success criteria for themselves. Once they have a set of success criteria, students shade in the middle column to show how well they think they will do on each area. This is a form of self-assessment and gets students to reflect on their own current skill level. The final column is for them to consider how they will self-regulate to ensure that they perform well in each area. You could add another section of this resource to get students to reflect and evaluate their performance afterwards.

6. Vocabulary for metacognition

It's always difficult to teach abstract concepts. Metacognition isn't something we can touch or draw, it's something students have to be aware of in themselves, and so it can be very difficult to explain with clarity. Language is crucial. I created this taxonomy years ago to help myself and my students to have the vocabulary to talk and write about metacognition in a meaningful way.

I am aware of myself as a learner – I can: **observe, identify, notice, recognise, monitor, assess, judge** and **analyse** my learning behaviours.

I can understand my work and make connections – I can: **identify, connect, compare, assess, remember, link, define, describe, categorise, differentiate, explain, extrapolate, interpret, classify, combine, contrast**

I can strategise: **predict, organise, improve, implement, create, plan, arrange, order, formulate, select, restructure**

I can self-regulate: **adapt, modify, improve, enhance, implement, initiate, deploy, engage, remember, control, monitor, prioritise, synthesise, notice, shift, reflect**

I can reflect on my performance: **consider, deliberate, scrutinise, evaluate, contemplate, acknowledge, examine, recognise, ruminate, analyse, dissect, explore, interrogate, probe, assess**

7. Schemas for metacognition

We know that the adolescent brain is a complex beast. There are some key factors which can negatively impact on how effectively young people learn. I outlined this in the following way in my book *How to Teach English Literature* (2019):

1. The brain is more emotional than it is rational. This means that students who are experiencing less stability (such as anxiety, uncertainty, distress or anger) struggle to encode information for learning. Happy, stable students learn far more effectively.

2. The brain thrives on making connections between new knowledge and existing knowledge. This means that students with less prior knowledge find it harder to create strong neural networks because there isn't as much there to connect new information to.

3. The brain likes to organise and categorise things. If information is presented to us in a clear, organised way, it is far more likely that we will remember it. Students who do not have the requisite learning skills or support to organise their knowledge, find it harder to store information in the long term.

As teachers, it is important that our teaching enables students to use their brains in the most effective way possible. That is what metacognition is all about. We should:

- Explain to students how their brains work and store information. You can use the overview of the learning process from page 32.

- Help students to make connections between new and existing information at every opportunity. Review and activate relevant prior learning before introducing anything new. You can do this by using quizzes, images, or anything else which will spark memory of previous knowledge.

- Help students to *organise* new information. Think of the brain like a computer with a big document folder. A well-organised document folder would have separate folders with titles and all the documents would be filed in the appropriate places. You would know where to find information about photosynthesis because it would be in a clearly labelled folder, and it would be linked to other similar folders in plant biology. On the contrary, a badly organised folder would have loads of disorganised documents, not all named properly and in a random order with no clear categorisation.

- We can help our students to organise their knowledge better and, though we can't guarantee what the brain will do with it, we know that using clear organisational structures during the learning process has a significant positive impact.[1] We can use:

Knowledge organisers: these are a one-page summary of all the key knowledge for one unit of work. They work best when they are visually simple and organised into distinct categories. These are effective because they present the brain with clear organisation from the outset. I like to show my students a blank knowledge organiser at the start of a topic with just the category headings, and get them to write down any existing knowledge they already have.

Showing students a knowledge organiser prepares the brain for the information which is incoming helps them to identify the characteristics of that information in order to organise it, encode it and embed it for long-term memory.

Timeline of apartheid in South Africa	Key people	Key global connections	Big questions
	Political vocabulary	Legal vocabulary	Exam response structure

Graphic organisers: these are often called 'concept maps' or 'knowledge diagrams'. They are a way to use symbols and shapes

---

1 It is important to remember that memory is complex and that this analogy is being used simply to explain organisation. We know that memory is actually reconstructive and that every time we return to a memory or add new knowledge, we re-write and adapt the existing knowledge that we have. To read more about this, see the work of Yana Weinstein: www.bit.ly/39MqmjD.

to express knowledge and ideas and establish the relationships between them. You can give students these structures in advance, or they can be trained to create their own as part of their own note-taking or revision activities.

WAYS TO ORGANISE: TYPES OF ORGANISER

Diagram by Oliver Caviglioli

Finding ways to help students to organise information themselves is critical. We can give them templates and model how to do this at first, but we should then use metacognitive strategies to train them to do this independently. These are tools which they should have in their strategy kit. In an ideal world, students would be in a lesson, recognise the fact that they are listening to key information, and then independently decide to take notes using their skills in creating graphic organisers, or using the Cornell Notes system. Metacognitive learners identify when *they* need something and are able to proactively make the most out of learning opportunities.

The final hurdle for organisation is time management. When students are left to work independently, they have to portion out the time they have and use it wisely. This is a life skill. Just like the resources above which support students to organise information, we need ways to train them to organise the time they have and make it count. In my first book, I shared a revision menu which I use to help my students to organise themselves:

Christmas Revision Menu

Remember to embrace struggle!
Everything should be from memory and independent.
If you look at your notes, change pen colour...

5 min activities:
- Explode a quotation
- Explode an exam question
- Character mind map
- Answer three quiz questions
- Five minute essay plan
- Write down 'A Poison Tree' from memory

10 min activities:
- Watch one of our class revision videos
- Write down all of the key plot events in *Macbeth* in chronological order
- Answer six quiz questions
- Test yourself using your flashcards – randomly chosen
- Annotate an extract and write a plan

30 min activities:
- Practice extract essay (timed)
- Practice part B question (timed)
- Practice transactional piece (timed)
- Find an interesting image online and plan a creative response

Resources:
- Revision clocks – set your own time limit!
- Extracts and essay questions (use for timed responses, quick plans, exploding questions, annotating texts)
- English department blog site

A one hour revision session could look like this...

Explode an exam question (*Macbeth*, relationships) (5 mins)

10 min break – go for a walk outside

Revision clock (Witches, Banquo, Duncan) (15 mins)

Practice extract question – *Macbeth* – random from pack (30 mins)

Macbeth revision video on YouTube (10 mins)

You could help students to organise their time and use this or a similar strategy as part of their metacognitive process:

E.g. Revise for the assessment on human geography next week

Comprehend: What am I being asked to do? What content will I need to revise? What can revision look like?

Connect: Have I revised successfully in the past? What did I do then? How can this time be similar or different?

Strategise: What is the best approach for me to take with my revision? How long do I have? How can I structure a revision session? How can I plan my timings and ensure that I keep to them? How long can I focus before I will need a break?

Reflect: How did it go? Was my revision plan effective? Did I plan useful timings, or do I need to change the strategy next time?

References

Bodrova, E. (2006) 'Developing self-regulation: the Vygotskian view', *Academic Exchange Quarterly* 10 (4).

Brown, P. C., Roediger, H. L. and Mcdaniel, M. A. (2014) *Make it Stick: The Science of Successful Learning.* Cambridge, MA: Harvard University Press.

Mannion, J. and McAllister, K. (2020) *Fear Is The Mind Killer.* Woodbridge: John Catt Educational.

Michalsky, T. (2013) 'Integrating Skills and Wills Instruction in Self-Regulated Science Text Reading for Secondary Students', *International Journal of Science Education* 35 (11) pp. 1846-1873.

Quigley, A., Muijs, D. and Stringer, E. (2018) *Metacognition and Self Regulated Learning: Guidance Report.* Education Endowment Foundation. Retrieved from: www.bit.ly/3u6zual

Vygotsky, L. (1978) *Mind in society: the development of higher psychological processes.* London: Harvard University Press.

Webb, J. (2019) *How to Teach English Literature: Overcoming Cultural Poverty.* Woodbridge, Suffolk: John Catt Educational.

Chapter 3
The classroom: case studies

This chapter offers a range of practical ways to train students to learn metacognitively. This process takes time and effort, but it is worth it. In this section, teachers share how they use metacognitive strategies effectively when teaching their students.

Zoe Enser

Previously a classroom English teacher for over 20 years, head of department and school leader in charge of improving teaching and learning, Zoe is now lead English specialist advisor for Kent with The Education People and an Evidence Lead in Education (ELE) working with the EEF across Kent. She is also the author of *Fiorella & Mayer's Generative Learning in Action* (2020).

Metacognitive reading

Reading in secondary school is a difficult topic. On the one hand, we expect a certain proficiency from our students. On the other, we are introducing ever more complex texts and requiring students to do increasingly complex things with them. In addition, we have students who will find the basic mechanics of reading a real challenge and may have less experience and proficiency in this than others. This is why modelling the metacognitive processes around reading became such an important practice in my classroom. I begin by recapping how we approach a difficult or complex text, highlighting links back to concrete examples of where they have done this previously and identifying the different tools we all have available to use. For example, I might remind them of how we might use prior knowledge of the text, type, the author or the topic of the text. I recap how we might then make some predictions around this and use cues from things like the title, images or subheading.

I will then model skim reading to remind students how we get the gist of the text, again activating their metacognitive processes so they are always thinking not only about the text, but about what they can do to tackle this. Noting this for them can also support the load on their memory as they consider how to approach these tasks. Once they are working independently, it is important they can still do this and know what to do should they find something difficult in the text and so repeating this process and modelling it is invaluable.

I will then go on to model how I build comprehension before moving towards analysis, annotating the text with questions, comments, patterns and phrases I notice which could be important. It is useful to have a line of enquiry for this, be that an exam question or one which I have devised again as a reader to direct my exploration. I articulate this to students as I go along, getting them to collaborate on the process, adding to what I have noticed or reminding each other what we need to do. This also includes modelling the reading back and forth in the text, something which they can find especially difficult, with time constraints being a key concern for them especially when thinking of exam conditions. However, what is most important here is that we build up to fluency and automaticity with this. As I noted at the start some students will be confident already in this, but as the challenge increases all students can benefit from this type of recap and modelling. If they understand the processes they are then in a stronger position to know how they can tackle those challenges, have the self-efficacy to believe they can do so and regulate what they are doing, identifying where they have not understood something and what they might need to do in order to do so.

Metacognition is a powerful tool in handing over the mantle to the students so they have the tools available to them to be able to work independently and move towards real expertise in the processes we perhaps take for granted.

Isaac Alabi

Isaac is a physics teacher and Deputy Headteacher (designate) – Curriculum and Professional Development. He is currently completing his NPQH with the Ambition Institute.

My first encounter with metacognition was at a former school where it was described as 'learning to learn' and 'thinking about thinking'. My former school thought this was a way to improve outcomes for students. Thinking skills were taught to students in tutor groups and students were expected to use these skills in lessons. Badges were given out by teachers when students 'showed evidence' of these skills during class activities, usually during group work. Guess what? There was no improvement in the quality of outcomes in external exams. It turned out that students did not learn more and teachers did not teach more effectively by approaching metacognition in this way.

At another school, I was presented with a challenge that will be familiar to science colleagues in many schools – there were a lot of passive learners in the science classrooms during practicals. Science is a practical subject and group work and discussion were a strong feature of many lessons. Students carried out practicals in groups of three to five, depending on the availability of resources. During practical work most students sat and chatted while the same one or two students did most of the work. How could we solve this problem? I decided to introduce a metacognitive regulation wrapper during group work. A wrapper is an activity that surrounds a learning or assessment task and fosters students' metacognition.

I set up practical groups and included one or two students who were more metacognitive in each group. In the middle of an activity, these 'metacognitive behaviour monitors' would stop everyone and give feedback on behaviours exhibited by each student in the group. I would then ask all students to reflect on their feedback and write down what behaviour they would work on in the second half of the activity. These are some of the prompts used:

While you have been learning, some students have been observing you as part of helping you to become a better learner.

Are you aware of the things you do during the learning process?

What do you know about yourself as a learner?

What conditions help you to be the best learner?

As the class got better at being aware of their behaviours during learning activities, more students were used as monitors. Below is the metacognitive monitoring sheet that was given to the trained student observers in each group during practicals/group work.

Name of observer:

Name of students	Observations before feedback	Observations after feedback

In my lessons, I used the questions below to model metacognitive regulation;

Before attempting a task (planning):

- Have I seen a question or task like this before?
- What strategies are available and what strategy did I use?

- What should I do first?

While completing the task (monitoring):

- Am I on the right track?
- How do I know I am on the right track?
- Do I need a change of strategies?

After completing the task (evaluation):

- What strategy worked well?
- What have I learned that I can use for future tasks?
- How can I memorise this strategy?

This helped my students to become more aware of their behaviours during learning and improved their ability to self-regulate in my lessons.

Over time, it became apparent that doing all of this while trying to teach new knowledge was too much for some of my students. I decided to focus on explicit teaching and only introduced metacognitive regulation after pupils had experienced sufficient practice and knowledge. In the metacognitive regulation phase during a series of lessons (this often takes place before students engage in independent learning in lessons), I used what I called 'learning stations'. At each learning station, all students collected questions that were designed to assess different aspects of learning. Sometimes during independent practice, learning stations had prompts to help students form a habit around how they should approach tasks. Students were sometimes prompted to consider the questions before attempting a task (e.g., 'Have I seen a question like this before?').

An example of a learning station grid

Learning station 1:	Learning station 2:
How confident are you that you understand the Big Bang theory? Explain the key words here: The Big Bang theory:	Using retrieved prior knowledge: List the electromagnetic waves starting with the EM wave with the longest wavelength. How does decreasing the wavelength of a wave affect its frequency?
After completing learning station 3: Write any formulae that you would use to calculate the speed of a wave:	**Metacognitive regulation:** What memory strategy did you use for the electromagnetic wave question? Did you succeed in correctly retrieving the EM waves in the correct order? How have you monitored how well you are learning in today's lesson?

Improving the way I implement metacognition in my classroom has had an outstanding impact on my students' outcomes at GCSE. The goal of implementing metacognition is to improve students' habits of self-regulation and, ultimately, better outcomes.

How do I now implement metacognition in my classroom?

What I have found most helpful is to structure my teaching to focus on cognition and direct instruction first, including modelling and metacognitive talk. Metacognitive talk of strategy, what strategies are available, why I have made certain decisions, what other options I could have used and why I did not use them. The end goal is to help students to do this on their own as they engage in learning and improving learning.

Implementing metacognition in a series of lessons follows this sequence:

1. Activate prior knowledge: during 'Do Now' and before a new knowledge is introduced, my students activate the prior learning that is needed for the lesson using retrieval practice.

2. New knowledge introduced in small chunks. The introduction of each chunk is followed by:
   a. explicit teaching of vocabulary.
   b. explicit instruction of task and strategy of new knowledge (metacognitive knowledge).
   c. modelling the use of strategies and metacognitive talk.
   d. guided practice.
   e. metacognitive regulation during independent practice.

Self-regulation at home

Teach your students about the forgetting curve, why learning is hard and how to minimise forgetting. My experience is that students find it fascinating and an understanding of how we learn often leads to a change in attitude to learning.

Have you ever wondered why your students may not like to complete homework or study at home? Learning is hard and engaging in learning at home is even more challenging when students have not been successful at it in the past. A lot of students do not study enough at home and, when they do, they often use revision methods that are simply inefficient. Explicit strategy instruction is one of the recommendations from the EEF guide on metacognition (Quigley et al, 2018). The work of Dunlosky showed that not all revision strategies are equal, some are more effective than others (Dunlosky et al, 2021). For students to use these strategies for learning when they are at home, they need to understand why. Why do they have to use these strategies? It is because of the forgetting curve.

I teach my students about the forgetting curve. I also explicitly teach my students about the different strategies that have been shown to be effective. As part of the explicit teaching of these effective strategies, I teach my students about the distinction between declarative and procedural knowledge. **Declarative knowledge** is knowledge about facts and things (so key curriculum content). **Procedural knowledge** is knowledge about how to perform certain activities (the metacognitive knowledge students have in relation to problem solving, analysis, reading, etc.). Why is this distinction important? So that my students can select the right tool for the particular task at hand. Knowledge of the forgetting curve and the strategies for learning that have been shown to be effective are both part of the metacognitive knowledge that learners need. Students cannot really become metacognitive or self-regulated learners without the knowledge of our subjects, the knowledge of how we learn and the different strategies that are effective for learning.

Nathan Burns

Nathan is a teacher of mathematics and Assistant KS3 Progress and Achievement Leader at David Nieper Academy, Alfreton. He is a former Metacognitive Implementation Lead as well as the founder of metacognition. org.uk, which offers metacognitive resources and CPD. Nathan is passionate about teaching and learning, and has researched, written about and delivered CPD on metacognition for several years.

In my years delivering what I hope is highly metacognitive teaching, as well as leading CPD and implementation across a number of departments and schools, it was actually Craig Barton who cemented my belief on the biggest barrier to implementation. Renowned for his work in mathematics, an answer in a Q&A on variation theory from Barton struck a chord with me. He was asked what to do following a disaster of a lesson where they (the teacher) had tried to implement a variation task. His answer was that the teacher should continue to persevere, that new strategies take time to implement and students time to adapt (Barton, 2021). Though my focus is on metacognition, my advice doesn't vary much.

The biggest challenge in my own classroom – and others who have introduced metacognitive strategies – is that it is a big change. Through developing our metacognitive teaching, we will naturally be challenging students to think harder. We're pushing them, often in an area that is complex, abstract and/or previously not covered. We may have encouraged students to 'mark their work in another colour and pick a target', but have we really challenged students to delve into mistakes, consider their knowledge of self, and develop high quality targets for themselves on a regular basis? Probably not. Students often push back at this. Quite often, students are confused or find the work extremely hard. Where we challenge students academically, it can sometimes lead to a pushback behaviourally.

So, how can you make metacognition work for you? When beginning to introduce a metacognitive strategy or change to your practice, choose an understanding class, not the one which needs your constant cajoling to stay on task in usual circumstances. Remember that becoming a metacognitive teacher is a marathon and not a sprint, so you don't need to be metacognitive with all classes instantly. Hone your practice with this trial group and be extremely careful in selecting a strategy that is appropriate in addressing an identified weakness of the group or an area that you want the group to improve (e.g. an exam wrapper following an end-of-unit assessment, see example on page 56-57), as well as ensuring that you scaffold the strategy as much as possible. For example, you may want to provide planning grids for students to fill in, directed questions that students answer, or a favourite of mine, key question cards that students use to quiz each other. This second point is key. Remember, even if you're not aware of personally being metacognitive, I can guarantee that you are. You work in education and are therefore constantly planning, monitoring and evaluating. Metacognition is second nature to you, so much so that you might not even be aware of it. Many of our students, however, are new to this. When you start shining the light on your expert metacognitive practice, remember that students will need a huge amount of scaffolding for all strategies and all groups to begin with. Make the strategy accessible and ensure that expectations and outcomes are clear.

Once you have dipped your toe in the water, you need to dive in. Metacognition will not make the positive impact that it promises unless it becomes a frequent and integrated part of your day-to-day teaching. A one-off, bolt-on activity does not suddenly translate your learners into metacognitive masters. Rather, continue to integrate appropriate metacognitive strategies across your lessons with a class, ensuring that they are frequent, appropriate to the metacognitive thinking you're working on, and well scaffolded. By providing students with continued exposure to metacognition, they will become familiar with the expectations and the hard thinking that comes with it.

So, what is the benefit of following this journey? Once metacognition is a frequent and well-integrated part of your classroom practice, you'll begin to slowly develop a class of students who are scaffold-free and using metacognition independently. Not just independently of you, but independently of the classroom as well. You'll begin to mould students who are consciously metacognitive. Students who understand the power of metacognition.

Sarah Dowey

Sarah is an experienced English teacher with a passion for literature. She is also a PhD research student in Education at the University of York. Her research interests include teacher attitudes to metacognition, and how metacognition can be used in the classroom to develop 'soft skills' and increase academic attainment. To see more of her work, you can find it at www.osf.io/vx7nr (Teacher understanding and awareness of the use of metacognition and self-efficacy in face to face teaching) and www.osf.io/rghjc (Metacognition, Self Regulation, and Academic Learning: a study of the role of metacognition and self-regulation in GCSE English Literature classes, student metacognition, self-efficacy and academic anxiety).

I approached Sarah through Twitter because her PhD research into metacognition in the classroom is incredibly exciting. There is relatively little work being done in this area by practising teachers and the early findings from Sarah's work are compelling. The following is an extract from Sarah's PhD thesis which outlines some of the key strategies which she has been trialling in the classroom.

Case study: Using a metacognitive approach to teach *Macbeth*

Context – the bigger study

This case study forms part of a larger study (Study 1), which is researching the effect of using a metacognitive approach to teach a GCSE English Literature text (*Macbeth*), and is currently in the data collection phase as this book goes to press. The aim of Study 1 is to investigate if teaching students with a combined metacognitive and knowledge-based approach is more effective in increasing academic attainment, self-efficacy, memory for quotations and in reducing academic anxiety than a purely knowledge-based approach.

Before beginning the main study, I wanted to trial the combined knowledge-based and metacognitive intervention in order to refine the content, if required, and to find out how useful participating students had found this method of learning. Basically, I wanted to pre-mortem the schemes of learning I had designed, before running them in Study 1, and to know if the students had found the intervention as beneficial as I believed they would! Following the intervention, all students completed an anonymous questionnaire, which I designed to find out how useful they thought the intervention had been.

Figure 1: The questionnaire completed by students as part of the acceptability study.

Side 'A'

Side 'B'

Case study: strategies and results

The strategies used in this case study can be broadly divided into two categories: teacher-led and independent. Although, to a degree, all the strategies used were teacher-led to begin with as clear modelling and instructions were needed to enable students to use and apply them. The division into teacher-led and independent strategies is mine, and categorises those activities into either classroom-based ones (teacher-led) or ones that students could utilise at home (independent). It is not meant to represent two dichotomous categories. Below are descriptions and results of the strategies that the students seemed to find most useful.

Teacher-led strategies

Live modelling: how to write an essay/mark student work/plan an essay

During live modelling, I work on a task that all the students watch me complete in real time while explicitly verbalising my thought processes so that they can understand *how* to construct their own work. Apart from eradicating the 'But how shall I start?' issue, live modelling gives students a valuable opportunity to experience a skilled expert share their expertise. To ensure that I have the students' attention throughout the process, I do not let them copy what I am writing as I model (I do provide a copy for them to refer to afterwards though). Instead, they have to remain active in the process, correcting 'deliberate mistakes' and suggesting vocabulary, quotations, improvements and different interpretations of the text when prompted to. As I construct my answers, I verbalised not only *what* I was writing but *why* I was writing it. This was so they could understand why I:

- crossed out some words to choose better ones.
- focused my language to explicitly refer to the question.
- selected tentative language to express my ideas.
- explained when to begin a new paragraph.
- showed how to write about structure; demonstrated how to use subject specific language (without feature-spotting).
- analysed multiple meanings and ambiguities in language.

In addition to modelling longer responses, I also took as many opportunities as possible to verbalise my thought process when tackling planning tasks, such as modelling *how* to write an essay plan and demonstrating *how* I assessed students' work. The latter was done under the visualiser and initially – to ensure students were comfortable with this – I would select a student and ask them if it was okay to share their work however, as the class became used to this approach,

I had an increasing number of volunteers. As I marked the work (the focus was always positive and considered what was effective about their work and how we could make it even more effective) I clearly verbalised my thought processes in evaluating what they had written and how they could improve, so students could understand *how* I was marking and what decisions I was making as I assessed it and *why*. As this developed, students became more adept at asking themselves the questions that I had verbalised when live writing, planning and marking, and consequently more aware during the process of writing of how successful they were in meeting the criteria.

The questionnaire results indicated that students viewed this explicit modelling as having a positive impact on helping them improve their academic attainment. Of these, modelling essay responses seemed to be the most helpful, with 47 out of 59 (79.6%) students self-reporting it as 'very useful', compared to 2 (3.4%) students who considered this method 'not at all' useful. In response to the question, 'What is the most useful thing (apart from subject knowledge and the success criteria) you have learned about how to tackle a *Macbeth* assessment?' teacher modelling of writing essays or being shown how to structure essays were mentioned 22 times. This included comments such as: 'The most useful thing is looking at one the teacher has made as they are usually very detailed and explains thoroughly what she has wrote and why.' Furthermore, a number of answers to this question also referenced specific strategies that students had been explicitly taught to help improve their academic marks during the live modelling process which they had found useful. For example: 'I learned what kind of quotations to include and how to analyse and link them to the play. Learning specific vocabulary has helped me structure sentences with more sophisticated language.' 'I have also learned to annotate a quote very well and get the most meaning out of it also to track chronologically through the play and the quotations', and 'How to annotate and pick out importance in certain pieces of text to secure a good answer.'

Live modelling also seemed to help students develop their academic self-efficacy (their confidence that they could complete an academic task successfully) with explicit essay modelling the most beneficial. 40 (69%) of students recorded it as 'very useful' compared to 3 (5.2%) who found it 'not at all useful'. Students also self-reported that being able to create their own detailed revision plans had improved their self-efficacy. 22 (38.6%) of students considered this strategy 'very useful' in developing their confidence in their ability to complete a task, in contrast to 7 (12.3%) of participants who deemed it 'not at all useful'. Considering that students self-recorded that teacher-led, explicitly modelled essay planning was one of the most effective strategies in helping to boost self-efficacy, it might be they had then transferred the skills learned in this strategy to their own independent essay planning skills, and that they were moving from novice to expert in utilising this strategy. Three student responses to the question, 'What is the most useful thing (apart from subject knowledge and the success criteria) you have learned about how to tackle a *Macbeth* assessment?' included references to increased confidence. One of these students wrote, 'I found learning how to structure the assessment by watching you or others who have got a high grade has boosted my confidence in how to structure a *Macbeth* assessment or any assessment. This helps me by making me more confident and understanding what it should look like.'

3-minute recall

Every lesson included one '3-minute recall' (3MR) section, which was developed from the idea of spending part of every lesson developing students' memory through regular retrieval practice, an idea adapted from Jennifer Webb's book *How to Teach English Literature* (2019). At different points in the lesson (specified by the intervention), students had to instantly stop what they were doing and complete the 3MR. Tasks included: 'List as many quotations as you can about the witches in *Macbeth*' and 'List as many quotations as you can remember about the theme of appearances vs reality in *Macbeth*' and aimed to increase students' memory for quotations in a low-stakes scenario, which did not increase academic anxiety. To ensure that students were not put under pressure during the use of this strategy, the number of quotations students remembered was not shared with either me, or the rest of the class. Instead, I used a number of methods to get feedback from students. For example, we focused on the number of quotations that were remembered as a class by rotating through the class, asking students to read out a quotation they remembered. The purpose of this approach was to make students more aware of and responsible for the amount of quotations they knew, as well as regularly exposing them to short quotations from the text. As we progressed through the intervention, I found that students became keen not only to beat each other by remembering as many quotations as possible, but also to improve lesson on lesson to beat their own previous scores, which they did!

The results showed that students perceived this as a useful strategy, which helped them improve their memory for quotations. Out of the 59 students, 33 (56%) rated it as 'very useful' and a further 23 (39%) as 'a bit useful'. Although only five students specifically mentioned 3MR as a useful strategy on the B side of the questionnaire ('3-minute recall as it meant we could never forget stuff'), a further 12 referenced it less explicitly as being useful with comments such as, 'writing out 10 different quotes from different characters in a lesson in a short space of time from memory' and 'going round the class, having to say a new quote'.

Student-led strategies

Dual-coded revision cards and spaced learning

Although both of these strategies were taught separately, in this study I had designed them to be used together to help students improve their memory for quotations. We briefly looked at the theory behind each strategy and then dived straight in with creating and using the resources needed for students to take home and experiment with this approach. Firstly, each student was given a list of 15 quotations they needed to learn for a character. They began by writing each quotation on one side of a revision card (one quotation per card). On the other side they had to draw an image that either represented or helped them remember the quotation. This could be literal, for example when given the quotation, 'Fill me from the crown to the toe top-full of direst cruelty', they might draw a picture of crown and a big toe. Or it could be abstract, such as a lion to represent the quotation 'brave Macbeth'. Lots of modelling was used to show students how to do this and I made it very clear that technical artistic ability was not a necessity – any student who has seen my homemade dual-coded revision cards can attest to that!

Once we had the cards, I explained how they could be used with spaced learning to self-quiz at home, or to get others to help with their quizzing. To do this (on day 1) students took their stack of 15 quotation cards, image side up, and tried to remember the quotation on the other side. If successful they put the revision card into pile 1, but if unsuccessful they were put in pile 2. The next day (day 2) they did the same, working through only the cards in pile 2 (the ones they hadn't remembered) but put them all back into pile 1 whether they remembered them or not. The day after (day 3) they began the process again from day 1 with all the revision cards until the end of day 5. They were only allowed to spend five minutes a day on this, with weekends off. As we worked through the intervention, we built up cards on all the main characters and each week we alternated which cards we revised. Towards the end of the intervention, we switched the focus to themes for spaced learning, rather than characters, to show how we could adapt our quotations to use in different examination questions. To do this I gave them a theme, such as ambition, and they selected the ten most relevant quotations from the cards (they had already made) to self-quiz with during the week.

Results from the sample demonstrated that the students found using dual-coded revision cards overwhelmingly the most useful to help them memorise quotations with 52 out of 58 (90%) students rating it as 'very useful' and a further four as 'a bit useful'. It was also rated as the most useful approach used by students during the intervention out of all the teacher-led and independent strategies they were shown to study *Macbeth*. In reply to the questionnaire instruction, 'Please list and explain any other strategies you found useful in helping you learn/remember quotations', 34 out of the 52 students (65%) who responded to this section included dual-coded revision cards as a useful strategy. Most students simply listed 'revision cards with pictures on' or 'drawing the pictures for the quotes' as being useful. However, others explained that it helped 'to use your own drawings to remember it better', or 'draw funny drawings so you remember them' and 'revision cards (with pictures) – I can remember the picture if it makes me laugh or looks unusual'. Three student comments about the least useful thing they had learn during the study mentioned dual coding. Two of these were because they had not found it useful and the other, 'because if you can't draw, sometimes you can't even understand what you draw'. Despite this, this student found making revision cards useful, 'as they help me learn the quotes I need to learn by testing myself on them nearly every day'. Additionally, one of the students who did not find dual coding useful did find that, 'Learning how to successfully carry out spaced learning was effective for me and really helped to improve my recall'. 12 students directly referenced 'spaced learning' as a useful strategy in their questionnaire response to listing strategies that helped them learn quotations, such as 'spaced learning – because it helps it stick in my mind'. A further 8 students made comments that referred less explicitly to spaced learning, but their answers appeared to suggest that they had found it a useful approach. Examples included: 'having them in different piles of which I need to learn' and 'split the quotes and learn them in parts'.

Skim reading examination extracts while highlighting key quotations

Although initially live modelled, this was a strategy that students quickly became adept at using independently. For example, before I live modelled a response to the question, 'What impression does Shakespeare create of Macbeth in this extract [Act 5, Scene 7]?', I modelled skim reading through the extract to highlight relevant quotations, while explaining how they would help me answer the question. I explained that I had done this because, practically, it helps me quickly find the quotations I need when writing my response; it helps me focus tightly on the question (so I'm not writing about the impression Shakespeare creates of Macduff); and, it helps me track logically through the extract and to also make links as I write.

The results showed that students found this simple strategy really useful in helping them improve their assessment marks with only 3 (5%) of participants recording it as 'not at all useful'. In contrast 25 (42.4%) answered that they found it 'very useful' and 31 (52.6%) 'a bit useful'. This strategy was included in the intervention to help students answer GCSE-style extract questions. For example, the *Macbeth* extract question in the 2019 GCSE English Literature Shakespeare examination was: 'Read the extract [taken from Act 5, Scene 1]. Then answer the following question: Look at how Macbeth speaks and behaves here. How do you think an audience might respond to Macbeth at this point in the play? Refer closely to details from the extract to support your answer.' It may be that students found this independent strategy the most useful in improving assessment marks because it could also be employed to improve time-management skills. In quickly identifying key quotations and then highlighting them in the text, students can direct more of their time to writing an answer that tracks logically through the whole text, responding closely to those parts of the extract that will enable them to answer the question. Previously, participants had struggled to track through the whole extract in 20 minutes, spending far too long reading the extract and not writing about the end of the extract and, as a result, losing marks. Although this strategy was directed at *Macbeth* extracts during the intervention, it is one of a number of strategies which could be potentially be used to help students efficiently identify and extract key information in other subject areas and text types.

Stacked bar chart showing the results of the self-reported effect of teacher-led strategies on participants in reducing academic anxiety, improving assessment grades, learning quotations and increasing self-efficacy post intervention.

Key of different codes used in the teacher-led strategy stacked bar chart

Teacher-led strategies	3-minute recall time	Modelling marking of student work	Modelling of essay planning and mind maps	Modelling essay writing	How to work out meanings of unfamiliar words
Reducing academic anxiety	TLSAA3MR	TLSAALSM	TLSAAMMP	TLSAAMLME	TLSAAUF
Improving assessment marks	TLSAM3MR	TLSAMMSM	TLSAMMP	TLSAMLME	TLSAMUF
Helping learn quotations	TLSQ3MR	TLSQMSM	TLSQMMP	TLSQLME	TLSQUF
Increasing self-efficacy	TLSSE3MR	TLSSEMSM	TLSSEMMP	TLSSELME	TLSELUF

Stacked bar chart showing the results of the self-reported effect of student-led strategies on participants in reducing academic anxiety, improving assessment grades, learning quotations and increasing self-efficacy post intervention.

Key of different codes used in the independent strategy stacked bar chart

Independent strategies	3 revision cards for self-testing	Highlighting key quotes	Checking on track in each paragraph	Spaced learning	Creating own revision plans
Reducing academic anxiety	ISAARC	ISAAKQ	ISAASC	ISAASL	ISAAEP
Improving assessment marks	ISAMRC	ISAMKQ	ISAMSC	ISAMSL	ISAMEP
Helping learn quotations	ISQRC	ISQKQ	ISQSC	ISQSL	ISQEP
Increasing self-efficacy	ISSERC	ISSEKQ	ISSESC	ISSESL	ISSEEP

A summary of metacognition and the classroom

You have just seen four separate teachers sharing nuggets of their work in metacognition. While their approaches vary, the same threads occur again and again. Questioning, modelling, links to cognition, activating prior knowledge, gradual building of skills and eventual removal of scaffolding. Getting students to regularly flex their metacognitive muscles is critical. Research suggests that if a neural system is repeatedly exercised, it will become more powerful (Bialystok and Martin, 2004; Bialystok and Shapiro, 2005). Metacognition is powerful. Frequent use of metacognitive functions through questioning, talk, retrieval, modelling, organisation, challenge and planning is the way to get the best performance out of students. More importantly, it will enable them to get the best performance out of *themselves.*

Key points to remember about metacognition in the classroom:

- Teaching metacognitively is about our everyday teaching behaviours. Metacognition is not about worksheets or bolt-ons.

- Students need to be trained in metacognition and that can prove a long process. Start with appropriate scaffolding and take it away over time.

- Use questioning based on comprehension, connection, strategy and reflection.

- Model as often as possible and ensure that you explicitly talk through your processes as you go, 'thinking out loud'.

- Model everything and break skills down into smaller component parts. Don't forget to model the work review so that students can be their own quality assurers.

- Metacognitive talk supports students to go from the external, to the private, to the internal.

- Metacognition is only effective when work is pitched at the appropriate level of challenge. Students can use metacognition to ensure that they are in the challenge 'sweet spot' and get the most out of their learning.

- Motivation is a critical part of learning. Students need to be willing to attempt challenging tasks and to propel themselves through lessons. They need to understand that lacking motivation sometimes is normal, but they can learn metacognitive skills to help themselves to improve their own attitude to learning.

- Feedback is the foundation of everything we do in the classroom. Students can't become metacognitive learners without expert feedback from their teachers.

- Students need the vocabulary to be able to express themselves metacognitively. We can support this with explicit vocabulary instruction, modelling, sentence stems and teacher talk.

- We learn better when information is clearly organised and when we have the skills to organise our knowledge and our time. A key part of the metacognitive process for students must be for them to be able to independently manage their time and the practical side of learning independently.

References

Barton, C. (2021) 'What Is Variation Theory', *Variation Theory* [Online]. Available at: www.bit.ly/32oWtll.

Bialystok, E. and Martin, M. M. (2004) 'Attention and inhibition in bilingual children: Evidence from the dimensional change card sort task', *Developmental Science* 7 (3) pp. 325-339.

Bialystok, E. and Shapiro, D. (2005) 'Ambiguous benefits: The effect of bilingualism on reversing ambiguous figures', *Developmental Science* 8 (6) pp. 595-604.

Dunlosky, J., Mueller, M. L., Morehead, K., Tauber, S. K., Thiede, K. W. and Metcalfe, J. (2021) 'Why does excellent monitoring accuracy not always produce gains in memory performance?', *Zeitschrift für Psychologie* 229 (2) pp 104–119.

Enser, Z. and Enser, M. (2020) *Fiorella & Mayer's Generative Learning in Action (In Action series)*. Woodbridge, Suffolk: John Catt Educational.

Quigley, A., Muijs, D. and Stringer, E. (2018) *Metacognition and Self Regulated Learning: Guidance Report.* Education Endowment Foundation. Retrieved from: www.bit.ly/3u6zual

Webb, J. (2019) *How to Teach English Literature: Overcoming Cultural Poverty.* Woodbridge, Suffolk: John Catt Educational.

Chapter 4

The teachers: Continuing Professional Development

School leaders need to see their staff through a range of different lenses. From a strictly business perspective with student outcomes as our focus, teachers are our most valuable resource. We must invest in their training and development so that they can effectively teach students. However, teachers are also learners in their own right. Leaders must see the intrinsic value in having staff who are skilled learners with the motivation and desire they need to engage in powerful development for themselves. So, we want our teachers to be acting as expert guides in metacognition in the classroom, but also to be students of metacognition in their own professional development.

This chapter will explore these questions:

- Improving CPD: how can metacognition make teachers better learners?
- Designing CPD: how can we train teachers in metacognition for the classroom?

Improving CPD: how can metacognition make teachers better learners?

1. The pitfalls

Continuing professional development. The clue is in the title. 'Continuing' – that means our CPD plans must go beyond the one-off Inset days. As senior leaders, we often make the mistake of assuming that teachers, by virtue of the fact that they are adults, are expert learners. We think that they will simply absorb everything the first time. *We are paying them, so isn't that how it should work?* I know I have been guilty of thinking this. I have planned CPD programmes which were too short and didn't support teachers as learners in the long term. I once led a whole school drive in vocabulary. We had training events spread over the course of the year, interspersed with accompanying briefings, meetings and opportunities to reinforce the learning. We also backed all of this up with Q&A activities, feedback and sharing good practice.

This was a program which was successful. By all measures, the work we did had a positive impact on student outcomes and staff practice. Cue self-congratulatory smiles from me. However, by the following September, it became clear very quickly that those gains were not particularly long-lasting. Once vocabulary was no longer the CPD focus, it was out of sight and out of mind. You could still see the surface level elements: word of the week displays, vocabulary lists in schemes of work, homework resources which had been planned the previous year. However, the real depth of understanding which I *thought* teachers had was not in evidence. Foundational knowledge of how vocabulary acquisition works was not underpinning staff practice on the ground. I was confused, an enormous amount of work had gone into vocabulary CPD but there had been little gained in the long term.

A huge amount of staff time and school resources are invested in CPD every year and I believe that this pattern is similar in many schools – how much of what we deliver to staff is truly meaningful and long-lasting? How many hours of training do we plan and deliver, only to see a minimal return? If you are a leader of staff CPD, a subject leader, or a teacher who has sat through these sessions, be honest with yourself: how much do you learn, retain and embed into your practice in the long term? 50%? 20%? Less?

What is the problem with teacher CPD?

When we want students to learn something for the long term and develop skills which they will use independently, we ensure that there is:

- Clarity of message
- Repetition
- Variation and exploration
- Retrieval and recall

- Modelling and practice of skill
- Frequent reminders and prompts
- Developmental feedback

How often do we see such a high standard of teaching when it comes to the education of our staff? Aren't they learners, too? Teacher CPD is about getting staff to adopt new behaviours or change existing ones. For example, if you want to develop oracy you might introduce a policy where teachers insist that students respond to questions in full sentences. In order for teachers to do this, they would need training in the associated theory and a range of strategies to help them to support students. This would involve a fundamental shift in the way teachers engage in dialogue with students. Someone who has spent ten years conducting questioning in a particular way will have a difficult time changing their ingrained habits and speech patterns in adopting such a policy. It is not as simple as someone in the senior leadership team saying, 'All students need to answer questions in full sentences', and this magically happening school-wide. Even a school full of well-intentioned staff who are all on board with an idea will struggle to suddenly change their behaviours quickly and for the long term.

We need to change the way we look at teacher CPD. If we take all the key principles of excellent teaching and maximise effective techniques for promoting long-term learning and skill development, we will have far greater results. Metacognition can play a significant role in teacher development. Everything I outlined in the classroom teaching section of this book can also be applied to teachers: their daily practice, improvement, development, and work in implementing whole school strategies and realising goals as a staff body. Metacognition can also support teachers to self-regulate in their work, understand their workload and become more efficient because they are aware of their needs and how they experience their work.

2. Long-term planning: the CPD curriculum

As I mentioned in the introduction, one of the issues with planning over a single year is that we get trapped in short-term cycles. This is a problem. We wouldn't ever plan a student academic curriculum as a single, standalone year. Plotted and sequenced properly, an academic curriculum is a five or seven-year cumulative work of art, upheld by core pillars of knowledge and connected in every direction by multiple threads and developing themes and concepts. We cycle through skills and knowledge, returning frequently to prior learning, building upon those foundations, and constantly elaborating on a tapestry of learning. Why can't we view teacher CPD as something similar?

John Tomsett (Tomsett and Uttley, 2020) wrote:

> 'In the last six years it has become plain to me that the quality of teacher learning is central to putting staff first. Any teacher, at any stage of his or her career, has to accept, continuously, the professional obligation to improve his or her teaching. Period. And once the teacher has accepted that obligation, the school has to accept the responsibility of providing the very best teacher learning opportunities. School leaders cannot just wish teachers to improve their teaching. School leaders have to put their staff's learning needs first.'

I am a big fan of a 'bookletised' curriculum. That is, having all the core content: reading, terminology, timelines, definitions, models, examples and supportive frameworks in one place so that students can work through something really powerful with the skilled guidance of their teacher. Booklets provide an opportunity for nuanced sequencing and for the student to gain a 'big picture' understanding of what is being taught over time. Whether learning is in a booklet or not, the power of having a strong curriculum and a delivery method which supports consistency is undeniably something we must strive for.

Why not take these key principles and embed them into our teacher CPD curriculum? Many schools use teacher reflective CPD journals, but we might push this further and create bespoke documents which support and guide teachers through their development.

What could go into a teacher CPD journal?

Overall school teacher development priorities: make the overall priorities for CPD clear so that teachers know what the big picture is. Teachers should be able to articulate the school vision for what great teaching looks like, and see how this informs the plans for CPD.

Knowledge organiser (for a particular area of CPD) with key reading, definitions, misconceptions:

Disciplinary reading knowledge organiser	
Key principles Disciplinary reading is about ensuring that all students can read in a way which is appropriate for the subject at hand. Reading in English literature means reading for deeper meaning: symbolism, structure and with a view to understanding something beyond the text. This is different to chemistry where reading is for understanding literal meaning, recognising how concepts link to one another, and ensuring that detail is not missed. On the surface, reading is reading. In reality, it is different in every subject.	**Common misconceptions** • Students need to read something they are interested in (e.g. football magazine articles). • Reading is only important in writing-heavy subjects. • 'Reading culture' is the job of the library and the English department.
Key terminology Tier 2 vocabulary Tier 3 vocabulary Disciplinary Polysemous vocabulary Homophone Translate/translation Etymology Morphology Orthography Phonology	**Big questions** ✓ Is reading an integral part of our curriculum? ✓ Do students have regular opportunities in lessons to engage with high-quality texts and develop disciplinary literacy skills in your subject area? ✓ Are students given regular opportunities to practise and develop skills to a high level (e.g. writing is fluent and expressive, performance is of high quality)?
Key reading Willingham, D. (2017) *The Reading Mind*. Quigley, A. (2020) *Closing the Reading Gap*. Education Endowment Foundation *(2018) Improving Literacy in Secondary Schools*: bit.ly/3v446L1	
Key strategies ✓ Regular core reading built into bookletised curriculum ✓ Teacher reading out loud – students are exposed to prosody, pronunciation, etc. ✓ Explicit vocabulary instruction using etymology and morphology ✓ Regular spelling tests (orthography) ✓ Support with pronunciation ('I say, you say') ✓ Framing questions ✓ Cornell Notes system and summarisation ✓ Chunking texts ✓ Prediction and contextualisation	

Key reading (articles, blogs, reports) to support the CPD focus:

I would highly recommend providing reading for staff which is relevant to their subject area. Presenting staff with research should be powerful because it gives them a 'why' – it shows them why something is important for their students. A CPD journal could be differentiated for subject areas to have a truly disciplinary approach to staff learning. This is an example of an article I might use for maths specialists, from Alex Quigley's work on reading (*Closing the Reading Gap*, 2020).

(DOMAIN SPECIFIC READING)
DOES READING *REALLY* MATTER IN MATHEMATICS?
In *Closing the Reading Gap* by Alex Quigley

Every teacher recognises that every subject is mediated by reading skill, but it matters in some more than others, right? Does it *really* matter that much in maths?
When I speak to teachers, or those school leaders responsible for aspects of literacy whole school, the refrain they often relate is that reading simply doesn't matter so much in maths. Perhaps maths teachers, beleaguered by past experiences of being led down the path of generic reading and writing approaches, are simply defending their hard-won teaching ground?

READING SKILL AND MATHEMATICAL VOCABULARY
Everyone recognises the unique language of mathematics that is separate to the everyday talk of pupils.
Maths is clothed by polysemous vocabulary (words that have multiple meanings) that can foster ambiguity and unhelpful misconceptions. Just a few include:

Prime, factor, base, angle, cardinal, common, proper, volume, difference

Not only that, some maths words are homophones (words having the same pronunciation but different meanings, origins, or spellings) with more common words e.g. *pi* and *pie*, *sine* and *sign*.

Even simple mathematical operations, like subtraction, is described in lots of ways in typical talk, such as **'subtract'**, **'minus'** or **'take away'**. Then you add in words like **'decrease'**, **'reduce'** and **'take off'**. Teachers are constantly translating the language of maths – not unlike a German or French teacher.

Researcher Andrew Rothery (1980) helpfully defined three categories of mathematical vocabulary:

1. Words which are specific to mathematics and not usually encountered in everyday language (e.g. hypotenuse, coefficient).
2. Words which occur in mathematics and ordinary English, but involve different meanings in these contexts (e.g. difference, volume).
3. Words which have the same or roughly the same meaning in both contexts (e.g. fewer, between).

A further translation challenge is how mathematics is represented in multiple ways. And so, when you read or write: $a^2 + (a + 2)^2 = 340$

The equivalent sentence in words to be read is...

'The sum of the squares of two consecutive positive even integers is 340.' (Schleppegrell, 2007)

Of course, many maths problems combine these representations, so that reading is a tricky, multi-faceted act for pupils. Careful, slow reading, and re-reading is often necessary to actually unpack the mathematical operations required by pupils.

In US research, perhaps unsurprisingly, it found that 'nationally, children perform 10% to 30% worse on arithmetic word problems than on comparable problems presented in numeric format'.

Teachers of maths will testify to the challenge of multi-step word problems. We can be confident then that reading in maths *really* does matter. Precision with mathematical talk will matter. Explicitly teaching on *'how to read like a mathematician'* could prove beneficial for those pupils struggling with word problems.

What other solutions can help? Explicit vocabulary instruction is likely one useful strategy. Keeping a glossary of mathematical terms, along with accompanying diagrams and representations could help (this may be particularly beneficial for EAL pupils too).

Being explicit and strategic about how you read – and re-read – maths problems is likely to help many pupils who are grappling simultaneously with learning the mathematics and the language of mathematics.

The deft interplay, flipping between everyday language to mathematical terms, and back again, by expert maths teachers will of course prove vital when teaching maths and the reading of mathematical problems or textbooks. 'Maths talk' will prove crucial for young children, whilst continuing to be vital at every key stage.

Reading matters in maths, more than most teachers, and pupils, may assume.

References

Rothery, A. (1980) *Children reading mathematics*. Worcester: College of Higher Education.

Schleppegrell, M. J. (2007) 'The Linguistic Challenges of Mathematics Teaching and Learning: A Research Review', *Reading & Writing Quarterly* 23 (2) pp. 139-159.

Resources to support teachers in working through and processing key reading content (Cornell Notes templates, prompt questions):

Key terms/ concepts/facts	Notes
	....
	....
	....
	....
	....
	....
	....
	....
	....
	....
	....
	....
	....
	....
	....
	....
	....
	....

Summary (In your own words...)

....

....

....

....

....

....

Scaffolded note-taking to support teacher developmental conversations (with subject areas or more focused conversations with fewer colleagues):

This is an adapted version of the resource for students you can see on page 37. This is a scaffold for teacher note-taking. The idea is that they would take their understanding from a CPD session and metacognitively reflect and make a plan for future practice. This could be more powerful if done as part of a discussion with a subject team.

Comprehension *What is the article saying? What strategies is it recommending? Does it challenge anything I already do in the classroom? Or does it confirm what I already do in the classroom? Or does it confirm what I already know, or support practice which is already embedded into my teaching?*	**Connection** *Is this similar or different to anything I have tried before? What do I think are the barriers to implementing these ideas or strategies? What might be the potential benefits? How could this relate most effectively to the demands of teaching my subject? How could this support the key improvement priorities in my subject area? How can this relate to my own personal targets?*

Strategy *When I have implemented new strategies before, what has been successful? Why was it successful? How can I ensure that I am successful this time? How will I start? After six weeks, what will be the key indicators that has been successful? How will I check and reflect on my progress over the course of the next six weeks?*

Personal reflection areas – following CPD activities, reading or following feedback

Improvement target
Strategy (what am I going to do?)
Reflection 1 *How did it go? How do I know? What would I change? Why? How will I change it? What went well? How can I sustain and build on that success?*
Reflection 2 *How did it go? How do I know? What would I change? Why? How will I change it? What went well? How can I sustain and build on that success?*

Reflection 3
How did it go? How do I know? What would I change? Why? How will I change it? What went well? How can I sustain and build on that success?

Subject team discussion
What did I gain from this process? What has been the impact (if any) on my students? What will I take forward or continue to develop? What lessons can we take as a subject team? How might this adapt our curriculum planning and delivery?

Try, refine, ditch

This is a resource which has been adapted from Amjad Ali's work on teacher CPD. Teachers use it to reflect metacognitively on their own goals and intentions during the training they are about to begin. They then use the 'try, refine, ditch' sheet to work through their learning in a practical way – what will help, what will they adapt in the future, what will they discard. To read more about this process, visit Amjad's website www.bit.ly/3oAHMGs.

Prepare yourself to learn:

- When have you been in a situation **like this before?** (e.g. a lecture? In-school CPD session?)
- How **motivated** do you feel for a whole day looking at screens? What could you do to help keep yourself motivated?
- What did you do to help you learn **last time?** Did it work? Why? Why not?
- What approach will you take **this time** to ensure that you get the most from the day? (e.g. using the Cornell Notes system, or writing down key questions as I listen)

Session title/ session lead	Self reflection: pre/during the session – areas you need to improve on/in	Action(s) to try	Action(s) to refine	Action(s) to ditch	Further info/reading
		By when?	By when?	By when?	
Example: *Behaviour management session*	*I need to be able to quieten a class down more effectively*	*Use of **So That** to signal to our students the point/ aim of the lesson being delivered, also to help explain the rationale behind the big questions'* / *Non-writing DNA to get students successful immediately on entry*	*Recall checks – use of timers and ensuring an 'easy' question*	*Anchoring language – avoid using the words easy/hard/simple/quick as these create an opt out and opt in nature of tasks*	*Planning for pitfalls – no books/equipment/ technology failing.*

Consider these questions a few days after the conference...

- How **effective** were you as a learner at the conference? **Rank yourself** from 1-10 where 1 is '*I took **nothing** in whatsoever,*' and 10 is '*I remember everything I learned and have a fully realised plan for implementing change in my classroom.*'
- Did your **strategies** for learning work? Why? Why not?
- What would you **change** next time to help yourself get more out of the day?
- How did your levels of **motivation change** over the course of the day? Did you do anything to help yourself stay motivated? Did it work? Why? Why not?
- What will you do to make yourself a more effective learner during future CPD opportunities?

Teacher self-study: rapid reflection

This resource is to support teachers to make tiny 'tweaks' to their practice, and to reflect on them in a detailed way over a series of lessons. I believe strongly that most 'okay-ish' teaching can become highly effective by employing a few judicious 'tweaks'. Most of the time, it's not huge elements of lessons which are the problem, it's the little refinements which make all the difference. For example, clarifying instructions, changing the way you stand or move, refining transitions between phases of the lesson, increasing or decreasing the level of challenge, altering and streamlining resources – all of these things can make a significant difference to the quality of our lessons. If we make a number of these tiny tweaks, we make marginal gains and our improvements multiply.

With this resource, a teacher:

1. identifies something they would like to improve in their teaching.
2. breaks this down into 1-3 'tweaks' which might help them with this improvement over four lessons.
3. can, after each lesson, write a very quick note in the box for each 'tweak' – how did it go? Did it work? What could be improved?
4. in the next lesson, can try to improve and reflect again.
5. by the end of four lessons, can reflect on the overall change to their practice. They might then continue the process for another four lessons, or change their focus.

The principle of this activity is that it is personal, very focused on tiny elements of classroom practice, and something which is incredibly swift. Short reflective notes – not something which should add to workload or be scrutinised by someone else. This is something a teacher can use for themselves.

Target:

Trial class:

Topic:

	Lesson 1	Lesson 2	Lesson 3	Lesson 4
Tweak 1:				
Tweak 2:				
Tweak 3:				
	Progress: Barriers: Focused, not finished:	Progress: Barriers: Focused, not finished:	Progress: Barriers: Focused, not finished:	Progress: Barriers: Focused, not finished:

What has been the most successful tweak? What has been the least successful? How did these tweaks change the student experience? What made the most difference to my practice? What will I carry forward? Why? What will I leave behind? Why? How do you feel about it? Why?

Target: More purposeful use of lesson time – no time wasted		Trial class: 8Y3	Topic: 1905 Revolution

	Tweak 1: Countdown routine for getting silence	Tweak 2: Swift transitions using clear instructions	Tweak 3: Using choral response for vocabulary instruction	
Lesson 1	Used '3-2-1'. Mostly worked. Some students not listening. Took a while for them to realise. Used behaviour policy to warn and sanction students.	Students taking a long time to move from one activity to the next – putting away mini whiteboards (MWBs) and pens, getting exercise books out is very noisy and time-consuming.	Used 'I say, you say' – difficult to get all students participating in choral response. Had to get individuals to repeat the response.	Progress: All three tweaks combined made the lesson more purposeful, even if not perfect. Barriers: Students need to practice with new routines. Focused, not finished: Repeat and refine processes until students are used to them.
Lesson 2	Used '3-2-1' but stood at the front of the room in exactly the same place each time (left of teacher desk) – worked a little better. Used behaviour policy to warn students.	Gave students instructions: 1. MWBs/pens in a pile 2. Exercise books out – date written 3. Waiting in silence for instructions. Improvement – still taking too long.	Repeated 'I say, you say' – used MWBs to get students to write out pronunciation phonetically first – how do you *think* it is pronounced? Used recall to get students to remember pronunciations from previous lesson.	Progress: Much better, faster transitions. Still work to do. Students know what to expect. Barriers: More practice needed. Some students not fully complying with instructions first time. Focused, not finished: Persist with current practice – it's working. Maintain high standards.
Lesson 3	Students now used to the routine. I am always saying the same thing and standing in the same place.	Repeated new routine – not fast or calm enough. Made students put MWBs out again and try one more time. Focus on efficiency and calm. Timed them. Much better.	Most students now responding confidently each time with 'I say, you say'. Not needing a reminder. I am doing it more frequently in lessons so they learn the routine.	Progress: Significant difference in student responses to routines and instructions – more efficient use of lesson time. Barriers: Still some students struggling with oracy and confidence. Focused, not finished: Keep practising and sustain this level with routines. Find further strategies for oracy.
Lesson 4	Sustained – it's working.	Used new routine – definite improvement. Still need to ensure calm and efficient transition – students still need reminders.	Working consistently in terms of student engagement – need to do more to help some specific students decode and pronounce words independently. Look into phonology – speak to SENDCO.	Progress: Lessons feel more purposeful – transitions are smoother. Barriers: Literacy barriers for some students – choral response is not the whole answer for them. Focused, not finished: Speak to SENDCO regarding strategies to support some students.

What has been the most successful tweak? What has been the least successful? How did these tweaks change the student experience? What made the most difference to my practice? What will I carry forward? Why? What will I leave behind? Why? How do you feel about it? Why?

Countdown for getting silence and the MWB/transition tweak have been really successful. Students have absolute clarity about what they need to do, and my own instructions have improved – consistency and repetition are key. I need to look at choral response for pronunciation – students all doing it, but some need far more support with oracy and confidence and in using new vocabulary in the classroom. I may adapt this strategy based on advice from SENDCO. I may also look into pairing 'I say, you say' with other oracy strategies such as full sentence response, and 'but, because, so'. Overall, I have felt less stressed and chaotic in my teaching since adopting these routines. It has helped me to focus on the content and skills I'm teaching, because I'm not worrying about transitions and student focus.

3. Initial teacher training (ITT)

During my teacher training I remember being constantly told to be a 'reflective practitioner'. It was the buzz phrase which all of our university sessions started and ended with. I don't think I really understood what it meant. At the time, I interpreted it as: 'Don't take feedback personally – get your head down and accept what people say, don't argue back.' You can probably tell from this that I didn't take criticism well in the early days! I wish now that I'd had the opportunity to dig into the idea of reflection a lot more. I often felt that it was a beige platitude – if I do what my mentor has said, or if I make sure I don't make that mistake again, that means I am being reflective.

Reflection is so much more than listening to other people's feedback or, worse, just doing what you are told because you think you should. True reflection is internal – it comes from an individual interrogating for themselves what has happened, identifying what went well, what did not, and why that might be. Reflection is about honestly examining your behaviour, your product and your impact. This can be something as broad as how effectively your scheme of work planning and teaching over time has prepared your students. But it can also be something as granular and minute as reflecting on a single exchange with a student, or asking yourself why someone still isn't grasping a concept and going back over your teaching language and approach. Now, of course, one can be coached to be reflective or we might have a colleague ask us probing questions to help us get to that reflection, but the real work has to be done by us as individuals.

Initial teacher training is a critical time for teacher learning and building strong habits as reflective practitioners. It is a natural place for metacognition to take root and – if we can ensure that it does – metacognitive skill will nourish teachers in their early years and into the future. Some ways of doing this are by embedding the questions and resources above in the CPD journal section. These key reflective questions and opportunities to make the most from training and reaching will have significant impact on the effectiveness of CPD for trainees.

Other ways we might support trainees during training is to enhance their support by including things like:

- **Metacognitive lesson study:** Practising teachers metacognitively narrate their own lessons. Sit with a trainee and watch a video recording of your lesson. At regular intervals, pause the video and talk through what you were thinking at that moment and why you did what you did.

  E.g. *I've decided to walk over to the back of the room because I can see that X students are starting to get distracted. If I walk over and stand close to them, they are more likely to stay on task.*

  Or, *I've just realised by doing some quick questions with the mini whiteboards, that a few students have misunderstood X concept. I've decided to follow this up with some probing questions where I get the students who DO understand to explain and explore it as part of class discussion. Once I've had a couple of students explain it, I'm going to ask some of the ones who didn't understand before to give me an example.*

- **Reflective marking and planning:** Practising teachers mark and plan and explicitly talk through thought processes as they go. Sit with a trainee and review a set of student work. Use the key errors, misconceptions and successes evident in the work to inform your planning of a future lesson. Talk through your thought processes as you do this:

  E.g. *The students have generally understood X well – this is interesting because I explained it using X analogy and that has clearly worked. I will need to ensure that I continue to build on this understanding – in the next lesson I'm going to vary that explanation and show them a couple of other examples of how X can be seen.*

  Or, *loads of students have forgotten to do X again! I'm not sure what I'm doing wrong – I've tried A and B already to combat this and it's becoming frustrating. I'm going to discuss this with the rest of the department at our next meeting to see what other people have found with the same skill.*

If experienced teachers model the reflective, metacognitive process with those who are new to the profession, we might foster the kind of meaningful work we hope to see from all teachers. Our work is immensely complex. It is important that, when we teach other teachers, we bare all and show them the messy reality. Making our thought processes explicit ensures that new teachers see that this isn't about pretty displays or perfectly neat exercise books. The best teachers recognise that progress isn't linear and that sometimes we take a few steps backwards before we move forwards again. Reflective practice is critical to moving forward in the classroom.

Designing CPD: how can we train teachers in metacognition for the classroom?

1. **Foundations:** Introducing metacognition to teacher practice is complex because it requires some fundamentals to be in place first.

Cognition. The most effective metacognition is built upon a solid understanding of cognition: how the brain learns, how memory works and how knowledge and skill develop over time. Learning is a messy process and we must be confident in our understanding of these core areas before metacognition can really have the impact we would like.

Feedback. Metacognition also requires really strong feedback practices to be in place. Students need regular meaningful feedback to support their own reflection on their learning. I wouldn't advocate launching work in metacognition in a school where there is still significant work to be done on establishing effective feedback.

Challenge. We can't reflect on whether something was difficult or whether we have been successful, if the activity in the first place was too easy or unreasonably hard. Curriculum planning and responsive teaching must ensure that the level of challenge is pitched right and, while this isn't possible 100% of the time, leaders have to be confident that students are being exposed to what Doug Lemov calls 'healthy struggle' as much as possible. If the level of challenge isn't right, metacognition will be relatively ineffective.

While these things won't be perfect all the time, it is critical that we have a strong foundation upon which metacognitive work can build. If I were a leader looking to introduce metacognition, I would look at the quality of teaching and learning in my school and consider:

- Do our staff have the knowledge, skill and confidence to start this new piece of work?
- Is this the right thing for us right now?
- Are we committed to doing this for the long term?
- Do we know what success looks like for us?

2. Time

The next key consideration is about long-term planning. As I said in the introduction, metacognition is not a quick fix. It is incredibly effective but requires time. Staff and students need to be trained and they must be supported to change their learning behaviours. This will not be as simple as embedding a non-negotiable starter activity in every lesson – it requires nuance. I would encourage leaders of teaching and learning to plan staff development programmes which go beyond a single academic year. Look at a two or three-year plan for introducing and embedding evidence-informed practice.

3. Priorities and making links

One of our challenges in leading teaching and learning is where we want to introduce something new, but struggle to maintain other key priorities at the same time. If you are introducing metacognition over the course of, say, two years, you might have one or two other priorities at the same time. Look at how those areas can support and enhance each other. For example, in running metacognition alongside a drive for disciplinary literacy, we might draw explicit links between the two. How do we model 'reading like a mathematician' using metacognitive teacher talk? How could students then reflect on this and create a maths-specific reading strategy for the next time they face a word problem?

4. Plan the CPD curriculum

Consider all of the core principles of planning a curriculum for students. All of these questions are absolutely critical when planning a development programme for teachers:

Sequencing

How do we sequence knowledge effectively? What do we start with? Why? What are the key concepts which need to be understood before moving on to the next thing? Where are our opportunities to explore ideas, practise and feedback?

In sequencing CPD on metacacognition, I would:

Activate prior knowledge: get staff to recall their understanding of the cognitive process, e.g. the work they have done around retrieval practice and the forgetting curve.

Connect practice: highlight the elements of staff practice which are *already* metacognitive. Many teachers use metacognitive strategies without realising it: modelling, reflection, student planning, following feedback, etc.

New knowledge: provide a very clear explanation of what metacognition is (see the examples on page 23), and then develop this by getting subject teams to explore more explicitly what this looks like in their subject (e.g. page 99).

Provide research evidence: use your judgement to provide staff with whatever research evidence you feel would be most appropriate for them. This should be easy to understand and something which makes the 'why' abundantly clear. I like to provide pre or post-reading to staff which is suitable to their subject area, but this might not be appropriate for all settings.

Explore possible strategies for the classroom: give clear strategies with examples of how they might work. This is not about saying 'you must do X', this is about giving some practical support for how strategies might be embedded.

Now pause. **Remember – subject relevance and specificity is everything.**

At this point, I would build in opportunities for staff to explore this in their subject areas. Make time in meeting schedules over time to talk about CPD and pedagogy as it pertains to specific disciplines. See the template above for the subject area discussion in the CPD journal (pages 99-101).

Reflect and return: in subsequent CPD sessions, provide opportunities for staff to give feedback on what has worked, what adaptations they have made and what challenges they have had. Ensure that there is an opportunity for meaningful reflection before moving on.

New knowledge and deep knowledge: when you are confident that staff have grasped the key concepts you started with, you might introduce new ones which build in sophistication. For example, you might have introduced 'comprehend – connect – strategy – reflect' (page 37) in your first introduction of metacognition, but later in the year you might enhance this by including Vygotsky's theory of external to internal metacognitive speech (page 44). You might also take existing knowledge which staff have now got a good grasp of and find ways to deepen and develop these concepts and their application. For example, we might have started by talking about the research around motivation and self-efficacy, but later in the year we could deepen this understanding by exploring the research around extrinsic and intrinsic motivation related to rewards. By carefully sequencing what we cover, when and how, we can build up staff knowledge over time, just as we would with the academic curriculum for students.

Challenge

How do we pitch challenge appropriately for all staff at different career stages? How do we adapt content and delivery for different groups? How do we make content appropriate for all subject areas? How do we adapt our approach for non-teaching staff where this is a consideration? How do we ensure that everyone feels as though this CPD is meaningful *for them*?

Does all of our CPD need to look completely different for every member of staff? No. But there absolutely must be provision and opportunity for individuals or groups to be treated differently where appropriate. I would advocate having some CPD opportunities where all staff are together so that everyone is getting the same message and can row in the same direction. This, however, does not need to be two hours in the hall with everyone listening to the same thing. You might have an initial 15-minute talk, followed by more focused work in specific groups tailored to subjects or career-stage. You might allow staff to self-select which training they attend based on session descriptions sent out in advance. If you subscribe to the CPD journal approach outlined on page 95-106, you might be able to link teachers' reflections to inform which sessions you provide in future.

Whatever you do, make it count and make it feel meaningful. Teachers want to feel as though their precious CPD time isn't being squandered by a system which has not considered them as autonomous, intelligent individuals.

Impact
What will success look like? What is our standard? What does a metacognitive classroom look like? How do we help teachers to take ownership of that? How will we know we have been successful? How will we track and diagnose progress over time? How will we provide interventions and support?

This final set of questions is particularly important because we must ensure that CPD is responsive. It is easy in the classroom to respond flexibly to student need because we see students relatively frequently, and there is a clear feedback loop and routine established. It is far more difficult to be responsive in staff CPD because we are so limited by time, number and frequency of sessions. We might create a beautifully structured CPD plan over a year, but that doesn't necessarily give us the space we might need to change course and respond to things as they come up. We need to be able to return to key ideas, address misconceptions and adapt appropriately. In order to do this, we should recognise that a CPD offer isn't just limited to designated CPD 'sessions' in twilights or Inset days. Much of our other teaching and learning or quality assurance activities can be powerful developmental support. For example, as part of a developmental process, use feedback after lesson drop-ins to discuss and reinforce key concepts from CPD. These are opportunities to fix misconceptions and explore ideas in greater depth and with a practical lens.

If you are designing CPD to introduce metacognition in school, either with all staff or a smaller team, you can find my CPD materials and templates on my website www.funkypedagogy.com.

A case study of whole school implementation of metacognition

Isaac Alabi

The benefit of starting small

Sometimes when new teaching and learning initiatives are introduced at a whole school level, not a lot of consideration is given to whether the initiative is the right thing to invest time and energy in or whether staff have the knowledge to successfully implement the initiative. At my school, we had seen the benefits of metacognition as some teachers in my school's science department had implemented it in their classrooms, but we were not sure whether this was a worthwhile initiative to pursue as a whole school strategy. What was the problem that we wanted to solve? Some of our students lacked motivation for learning and subsequently did not do very well in assessments. In lessons, these students often switched off and did not do much revision at home.

Why metacognition? The 2018 EEF teaching and learning toolkit identified metacognition as having a high impact for very low cost, based on extensive evidence. Metacognition and self-regulation approaches have consistently high levels of impact, with pupils making an average of seven month's worth of additional progress.

Once we decided that metacognition and self-regulation was an initiative that was worth pursuing, we decided to start small. In conversations with my headteacher, I explained that it was better to trial this in the science department, where I was head of department, to see what lessons could be learned and how whole school implementation could work. Another reason was that we wanted students to spread the 'good news' of the difference that metacognition and self-regulation was making to their learning. All science teachers were trained on how to support students to be metacognitive in lessons. During this time, we had a few school leaders visit from other schools as news of how we were implementing metacognition in the science department had spread. Ofsted visited my school some months after we implemented metacognition and self-regulation in the science department and wrote, 'Where teaching is strong, as in science, pupils develop their knowledge and deepen their understanding of the topics they study. Teaching in science has a convincing focus on how pupils learn, which is leading to pupils' thinking and understanding being fully developed.'

Trialling metacognition in the science department provided us with insight into how best to introduce this on a whole school level. Colleagues in other departments heard about the work that was being done in the science department through students and science colleagues and were intrigued.

Whole school introduction to metacognition

I introduced metacognition and self-regulation to staff during one of our Inset days and got a round of applause at the end of the over-an-hour's session. How did I introduce metacognition? I taught a lesson in which staff were my students. I am a physics teacher, so I taught a physics topic. The topic was electromagnetic waves. The purpose of this lesson was two-fold. First, I wanted staff to experience the EEF guide on implementing metacognition and self-regulation in the classroom. Second, I wanted to show how the implementation of metacognition supports effective teaching and learning.

Metacognition works well when challenge is planned into lessons as this challenge and the success experienced is what motivates learners to use their metacognitive knowledge and skills. After introducing the purpose of the lesson and the learning outcome, I proceeded to discuss the different strategies that we use for memorisation. I asked colleagues what their most effective memorisation strategy was and challenged them to assess its effectiveness by memorising a series of numbers. I encouraged staff to try other strategies if they were not successful with their chosen strategy. I then wrote the names of the electromagnetic waves on the board and asked them to memorise these using the strategy that they were successful with. Lots of comments and feedback at this point from colleagues came in on how easy it was to name the waves in the correct order. I checked for understanding and informed colleagues that I would assess their memorisation in 15 minutes.

For learners to be motivated in lessons, they need to be successful with learning – they need to be successful as quickly as possible. For learners to be successful, knowledge needs to be presented in small chunks and the cognitive load of learning considered. I planned for my colleagues to hold the names of the electromagnetic waves in their long-term memory as I taught the characteristics of these waves. This information helped colleagues to pay attention and better understand the new information that I taught to them. In the middle of the lesson, I asked science colleagues that had been assigned to each group to monitor colleagues as they engaged in the lesson to give them feedback on their behaviour during the lesson process. You can imagine what followed, lots of cackling, laughing and curiosity from colleagues about their behaviour during the learning process. In the second part of this lesson, colleagues paid more attention and showed better learning behaviour. Attention is the gateway through which information enters our working memory. Better learning behaviour improves attention.

As part of this lesson, I also taught how to engage in self-regulation during independent practice.

Teaching and learning framework based on metacognition

Following this Inset session, I asked colleagues to try this way of teaching in their subjects and their classrooms. A colleague who taught philosophy and ethics implemented this in their classroom and was excited to share what difference it made to her pupils. Other colleagues did the same in a way that worked for their subjects and were happy to share the success of the implementation.

We then shared a whole school teaching and learning framework based on metacognition and self-regulation. The framework was adapted from the EFF guide on metacognition.

Our teaching and learning framework:

- ☐ Activate prior learning (Do Now tasks and during lessons/sequence of lessons)
- ☐ Introduce new knowledge in small chunks. For each small chunk...

    1. Clearly explain new knowledge using dual coding where possible.

    2. Model new knowledge and engage in metacognitive talk – learners are novices at this point.

    3. Check for understanding

    4. Guided practice: 'I do, we do, you do'

- ☐ Independent practice (metacognitive regulation)
- ☐ Structured reflections

Professional development using research groups

To support the implementation of our teaching and learning framework, we introduced research groups. A research group is an opportunity for colleagues from different subject areas to meet regularly to read and consider research evidence on their chosen focus, reflect on their learning and their current practice and decide on what change they would like to make to their practice. Each research group had at least a colleague from each subject area. Department sessions often followed these research group sessions to encourage conversations about engaging with research and improving pedagogical content knowledge in subjects.

There were four research groups:

- Retrieval practice
- Spaced learning
- Cognitive load theory
- Deliberate practice

There was a group for heads of department to encourage shared understanding and language around the teaching and learning framework. I made a booklet for each research group and a copy was given to each member of each group. There were pages in each booklet for colleagues to write their reflections and plan what they would do with their new knowledge. Colleagues were also encouraged to visit lessons to support and celebrate the learning of their co-learners.

Subject level curriculum

The next phase of our implementation of metacognition and self-regulation was curriculum development. As a school, we moved forward with our 'masterplan' by asking subjects to consider how knowledge had been organised and sequenced and whether this had been done in a way that helped students to access their long-term memory quickly and efficiently.

Ofsted mentioned the need to 'integrate new knowledge into larger concepts'. This is schema development. A schema, as we know, is a cognitive framework or concept that helps to organise and interpret knowledge.

- Schema influences what we pay attention to.
- Schema impacts how quickly we learn.
- Schema allows us to think quickly.

Implications of our T&L framework for subject curriculums.

- Overlearning through extensive practice. For overlearning to take place, we will need to;

Plan sufficient time into the curriculum for extensive practice in lessons (how long will it take a student (SEND especially) to master this?

What about pause lessons (When? How many?)

What knowledge do you need to teach and which can you leave out?

What curriculum model should you use?

- Modelling everything (new knowledge): Allows for metacognitive talk and apprenticeship.

- Clear and efficient explanations.

What are the most efficient pedagogies?

How many colleagues have a useful knowledge of these pedagogies in your subject area? What pedagogy works well for what topic?

- Self-regulation: Teach students how to plan, monitor and review learning during independent practice.
- The sequencing of the curriculum should help students to make meaning of knowledge.
- Activating prior knowledge should be designed into the curriculum.

References

Education Endowment Foundation (2018) 'Metacognition and self-regulation', *Teaching & Learning Toolkit*. Retrieved from: www.bit.ly/3xP8hMs

Quigley, A. (2020) *Closing the Reading Gap*. London: Routledge.

Tomsett, J. and Uttley, J. (2020) *Putting Staff First*. Woodbridge, Suffolk: John Catt Educational.

Chapter 5
What does the theory say?

Most classroom teachers do not have the time or the inclination to wade through reams of academic writing – teaching is intricate and time-consuming enough already. Good leadership of evidence-informed teaching and learning recognises that teachers need to engage with research in a way which is purposeful, appropriate for their context, and so that there is a clear link between theory and practice. My aim in this book has been to provide that link. As a research lead in a secondary school, I do the reading and research so that I can filter, contextualise and disseminate information to staff in a way which will be useful and supportive.

Teachers who want to take that reading forward can do so, but those who want to remain classroom focused are able to do so in the knowledge that their training and school policy is informed by robust evidence.

This book is firmly rooted in academic research around metacognition, but I have tried to keep most of the technical side of psychology, cognition and complex terminology to a minimum in favour of practical guidance for the classroom.

If you would like to explore this side of the research in more detail, here are some key texts and researchers to get you started.

Flavell, 1979
'Metacognitive knowledge is one's stored knowledge or beliefs about oneself and others as cognitive agents, about tasks, about actions or strategies, and about how all these interact to affect the outcomes of any sort of intellectual enterprise. Metacognitive experiences are conscious

cognitive or affective experiences that occur during the enterprise and concern any aspect of it – often, how well it is going.'

Flavell, J. (1979) 'Metacognition and cognitive monitoring: A new era of cognitive-development inquiry', *American Psychologist* 34 (10) pp. 906-911.

Hartman, 1998

'Metacognition is especially important because it affects acquisition, comprehension, retention and application of what is learned, in addition to affecting learning efficience, critical thinking and problem solving. Metacognitive awareness enables control or self-regulation over thinking and learning processes and products.'

Hartman, H, J. (1998) 'Metacognition in Teaching and Learning: An Introduction', *Instructional Science* 26 (1/2) pp. 1-3.

Michalsky, 2013

'Comprehension questions help learners understand the task's or problem's goals or main idea. Connection questions prompt learners to understand the task's deeper-level relational structures by focusing on prior knowledge, and by articulating thoughts and explanations. Strategy questions encourage learners to plan and select appropriate strategies and to monitor and control their effectiveness. Reflection questions play an important role in helping learners evaluate their problem-solving processes by encouraging learners to consider various perspectives and values regarding their solutions.'

Michalsky, T. (2013) 'Integrating Skills and Wills Instruction in Self-Regulated Science Text Reading for Secondary Students', *International Journal of Science Education* 35 (11) pp. 1846-1873.

Winne, 2017

SRL in four phases: 'In the first phase, the learner searches the external environment plus her memory to identify conditions that may have bearing on a task she is about to begin. This information represents context as the learner perceives it. In phase two, the learner forges goals for working on the task and drafts plans to approach those goals. Phase three is where work begins on the task itself.

Throughout all three of these phases, the self-regulating learner monitors information about (a) how learning was enacted using cognitive operations (e.g. SMART processes), study tactics and learning strategies; and (b) changes in the fit of internal and external conditions to various standards. For example, after mapping external conditions, the learner may judge she has only moderate efficacy and forecasts she will need help. Searching her store of knowledge and judging she is not very well equipped for this task, she becomes slightly anxious and sets a goal to seek help from others. A plan is designed to seek help that is either just in case, e.g. texting a friend to see if he will be in the library during study hall in the afternoon; or just in time, e.g. texting her friend at the moment need arises. Each plan, not yet enacted, is monitored for whether it seems it will sufficiently allay her anxiety. If not, an adaptation may be constructed.

Phase four of Winne and Hadwin's model of SRL is where learners elect to make substantial changes in their approach to future tasks.'

Winne, P. H. (2017) 'Cognition and Metacognition within Self-Regulated Learning', *Handbook of Self-Regulation of Learning and Performance*. Abingdon: Routledge. Retrieved from: www.bit.ly/3ei7jAo

Shimamura, 2018

'Knowing about what we know is a process that psychologists call metacognition (meta is Greek for "about" or "beyond"). It involves monitoring learning processes, such as asking whether new material was actually understood, and controlling future processes, such as deciding if more study time is required. The generation effect is both a means of reinforcing learning and a way of monitoring whether you have learned the material.'

'[...] instilling interest in the learner (motivate), selecting relevant information (attend), integrating new information with existing knowledge (relate), retrieving the information (generate), and monitoring success in learning (evaluate)'

Shimamura, A. (2018) *MARGE: A Whole-Brain Learning Approach for Students and Teachers*. Available at: www.bit.ly/3ei8r76

Chapter 6
Notes on leadership

The why

Done well, metacognition is transformational. It is different to any other area of pedagogy because it has the potential to enhance the life of a child beyond the academic sphere. A young person who has learned to be metacognitive can apply those principles to regulate their emotions, face adversity, adapt and strategise in response to challenge. Metacognition is fundamentally about our understanding of ourselves and that is where its power lies. Once we understand ourselves, we are able to be intentional about the ways in which we use our energies.

For me personally, this intentionality is critical to everything. I went through my entire school career, my English degree and teacher training without ever knowing that I was dyslexic. I was diagnosed when I was an NQT in my first ever school. Over the course of my education, I struggled with reading. I could read and my understanding of texts was good, but I was very slow. My first week at university was a nightmare. Dickens week. I was utterly overwhelmed by the sheer quantity of it and terrified that I seemed to be the only person on my course who was failing to get through the content quickly enough. I realise now that I got through my GCSEs, A Levels, degree and PGCE because I had developed a range of quite sophisticated coping mechanisms. I had independently strategised my way through my barriers so that I could keep pursuing something I loved. Everything from reading rulers to pre-reading questions to complicated note-taking systems and colour-coding – I found a way through. This was metacognition. Before every writing assignment I made a plan, scheduled my reading, found ways to read what was important and leave the rest (because I simply could not read everything in the time I had). I reflected on how I was managing, changed my approach and continued to hone my practice. As a professional adult, I aim to be intentional in everything I do. I use my increasingly developed understanding of myself to ensure that I make the most of my skill set and make up for my deficiencies. As a dyslexic English teacher, I always do my marking first thing in the morning when I'm fresh – I skim read first for technical accuracy so that I'm not trying to see grammar and literary content all at once. Metacognition has enabled me to make the most of what I've got. While this isn't always successful, I know I am more effective when I have time to reflect, strategise and regulate my behaviours.

As leaders in schools, our job isn't just about student data outcomes. It's about their adult potential. A set of exam results can only open the door – young people must be equipped to succeed in new situations without the school being there to pick them up, give them feedback and then let them practice again. School environments are wonderful, nurturing places, but we have a duty to send our young people out in the world with the tools to fend for themselves. To return to a cheesy metaphor from the introduction of this book, metacognition can take baby birds and turn them into unicorns.

This is all great in theory, but what does this look like on the ground?

Quality of education is a pretty nebulous concept at the best of times, so how does a leader responsible for quality assurance of teaching and learning judge whether metacognition is embedded in a meaningful way across school? And how do we ensure that we are thinking beyond just the surface level of activities in lessons? Our work as educators can go so much further than that. Schools can build core pedagogical principles into every level of their work. In my own school, I look to see metacognition in classrooms but also in our thought processes, curriculum vision, leadership meetings and team dynamics.

I make no attempt to tell other teaching and learning leaders how to judge or track the quality of education in their schools – such decisions are highly context specific. What follows is a bank of questions which might prompt leaders to interrogate their practice and direct lines of inquiry.

Curriculum

I often hear the phrase 'a curriculum is only as good as the delivery.' To some extent this is correct – a great curriculum becomes a mediocre one if it is limited by poor teaching. Teaching, however, is not the only consideration here. Students have to meet us part of the way. A class full of baby birds will only ever be able to regurgitate things their teacher has handed to them. This means that a curriculum can only be as good as the actual learning which is taking place. A great curriculum needs learners who can take ownership and make the most of excellent teaching.

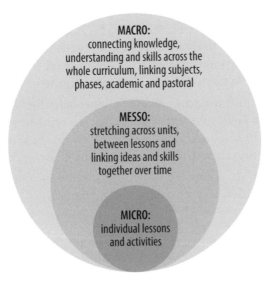

As leaders looking at the quality of education, therefore, we can't just look at what teachers are doing. We should be looking at what students are doing. We should ask ourselves:

Micro level

☐ What does a good lesson look like? Are we thinking about what the teacher is doing more than what the students are doing?

- ☐ Are students actively engaging in their learning (like, really), or are they passive participants in their own education? *Unicorns are often quiet – they are busy. You will need to speak to them. Do not interpret silence as lack of engagement.*

- ☐ Are students doing the thinking for themselves? Are teachers modelling that thinking?

- ☐ Can we see metacognition at play at a micro level through individual lessons and reflection activities?

Messo level

- ☐ Are key metacognitive ideas used across units, between lessons and as part of sequencing?

- ☐ Are students able to articulate how ideas are threaded over topics, and how skills develop over time?

- ☐ Are students actively making links between lessons and activities? Can they tell you when they last did something like this? What they learned from it and how they are approaching it this time?

- ☐ Is the learning metacognitive? (e.g. it pervades the entire classroom, it is not a bolt-on) Are students reflecting on their performance in things like recall activities, written work, practical work? *Unicorns aren't always successful, but they are always asking 'why' and 'how'.*

- ☐ Can you see knowledge and skills building over time, where metacognition and self-awareness are the 'glue'?

Macro level

- ☐ Are teachers working as a team across the school – referring to each other's subjects – aware of topics which overlap and complement one another?

- ☐ Is it clear that students see learning as something which is both disciplinary and personal? Can they tell you where skills and knowledge intersect across their whole curricular experience and where there are clear distinctions? *Unicorns understand nuance.*

- ☐ Is your curriculum interconnected in a meaningful way, or do you just have some pretty 'road maps'?

☐ Does your classroom culture move beyond those walls and out into the wider school? Do your non-teaching staff understand your teaching and learning policy? Do they know what your curriculum looks like and the rationale behind it?

☐ Can you see metacognitive principles in place in your behaviour/ restorative activities? In transition? In work with parents? In careers education? In your TA team? In your SEND work? With EAL students? *Unicorns exist in every cohort.*

☐ Are you utilising your entire team? Consider the power of having everyone rowing in the same direction.

Leadership structures

☐ Do we have helpful systems in place to support the development of teachers *over time*?

☐ Could our staff teams use metacognition to aid their effectiveness? Can it have impact when used in a group? (E.g. subject departments, pastoral teams, senior leadership team, temporary project teams, can they use: 'comprehension, connection, strategy, reflection'?)

☐ Are our leaders openly metacognitive? How can we visibly model those principles as senior leaders for staff and students?

☐ How might metacognitive question frameworks support line management and performance management?

☐ How might metacognitive frameworks support planning for school improvement?

☐ **Does the leadership team openly and honestly reflect on its successes and areas of weakness?** (Hint: if the majority of staff aren't managing to do something well, that is often a wider system or leadership problem, not the fault of the staff.) *Unicorns are honest with themselves, even when it's difficult to admit uncomfortable truths.*

Conclusion

To draw upon the words of Louise Saukila from the opening of this book, 'the brain and its ability and capacity to learn never ceases to amaze'. In teaching, we attempt to help young people make the most of their brain's enormous potential. We know that the brain is capable of incredible things, that the memory and function of a grown adult is so complex and developed that even our most advanced science cannot explain all of it.

I often think that teaching is a job of faith. We engage in a constant attempt to develop and nurture something which is, ultimately, invisible to us. We do our part, hoping that something is happening for the student, that they are taking it in and that it will become part of their world. Isn't it critical, therefore, that we teach students how to *use* those brains? Isn't it incumbent upon us to give them not only the knowledge and skills on our curriculum, but also the *tools* they need to 'drive' their brain in the most effective, efficient way possible?

I hope that this book has shown you that metacognition is an incredibly simple way of framing your teaching. No bells and whistles required. This is about developed, reflective questioning, appropriate sequencing and a considered approach to feedback.

Take your hesitant, uncertain baby birds and make some unicorns.